Child Neuropsychology i

Emilia Misheva

Child Neuropsychology in Practice

Perspectives from Educational Psychologists

Emilia Misheva
London, UK

ISBN 978-3-030-64932-6   ISBN 978-3-030-64930-2   (eBook)
https://doi.org/10.1007/978-3-030-64930-2

Cover pattern © John Rawsterne/patternhead.com

This Palgrave Macmillan imprint is published by the registered company Springer Nature Switzerland AG.
The registered company address is: Gewerbestrasse 11, 6330 Cham, Switzerland

ACKNOWLEDGEMENTS

I am indebted to the participants who took part in the research that has informed this book for their invaluable contributions and insights—I am truly grateful for their time and willingness to share their views with me. I would also like to thank the supervisors of my doctoral research—Prof. Andy Tolmie and Dr Tom Connor from the UCL Institute of Education, for their unwavering support. Additionally, I would like to express my gratitude to Dr Jane Hood, for her insightful advice, comments and guidance. Finally, I would like to extend my gratitude to Grace Jackson, Jo O'Neill and the team at Palgrave for their support, professionalism and enthusiasm for this project.

CONTENTS

LIST OF FIGURES

INTRODUCTION

NEUROPSYCHOLOGY AND EDUCATIONAL PSYCHOLOGY: AN UNEXPLORED RELATIONSHIP

The relationship between educational psychology and neuropsychology in the UK is a largely unexamined one, with only a small number of academic texts having attempted to address this knowledge gap in the past 20 years. One such attempt was made in 2005, when the British Psychological Society published a special issue of its *Child and Educational Psychology* journal (Gibbs, 2005), which focused specifically on neuropsychology. While this publication was seen by some as an expression of the increasing awareness of the links between neuropsychology and education (Harrison & Hood, 2008), only three of the published papers focused specifically on the link between the two disciplines and just 1 out of the 25 contributors was a practitioner EP, with the remaining authors being academics or clinical psychologists.

This tendency can also be observed in more recent academic texts, such as Child Neuropsychology: Concepts, Theory, and Practice (Reed & Warner-Rogers, 2009), where just one chapter was authored by an EP and focused on child neuropsychology and education. At the same time, education has been highlighted as a key focus area during the recovery of children with neurological conditions such as acquired brain injury (Slomine & Locascio, 2009), with EPs being amongst the key professionals involved in the ongoing support and monitoring of the educational needs of those children and young people (Ball & Howe, 2013).

The lack of representation of the educational psychology perspective in neuropsychological research and academic texts can be partially attributed to external factors, such as the proportionately higher number of clinical and academic psychologists working in neuropsychological settings or research (Specialist Register of Clinical Neuropsychologists, 2020); however, it is also important to consider the potential role of intra-professional factors that may have contributed to this imbalance. Historically, some academic commentators have associated the neuro-disciplines with overly medical and within-child models of thinking, and have questioned their applicability to educational psychology practice (Mayer, 1998). Bruer (1997), for example, referred to attempts to relate cognitive neuroscience to education as "a bridge too far". Similarly, Hood (2003) spoke about a "fear of being accused of exclusionary practice", particularly in relation to the inclusion of neuropsychological content on initial EP training courses. From this perspective, EPs' involvement and interest in neuropsychology-informed practice and research can be seen as having implications for their professional identity. More specifically, if EPs are encouraged to move away from individualistic, within-child models of working to more systemic ones (Noble & McGrath, 2008; Wilding & Griffey, 2015), an interest in neuropsychology may be seen by some as being incongruent with the core EP values and rejection of "within-child" models.

Hood (2003), however, argued that neuropsychology can enhance and complement EP practice and formulations, by offering a more detailed interpretation of how child brain development is linked to cognitive function, as well as how it is influenced and moderated by individual, environmental and systemic factors. She argued that this detailed information can then be used systemically, to enable the adults working with the child to make the necessary systemic and environmental adaptations, tailored to the child's individual needs. Paediatric neuropsychology and its applications to educational psychology thus appear to be subject to debate; however, up until this point, this relationship has not been examined empirically, with the most recent opinion papers dating back to nearly 20 years ago.

Similarly, little is known about the specialist role of EPs who work in neuropsychological settings such as brain injury or epilepsy services. One of the few publications looking at this specialist role is a book chapter written by an EP also practising as a neuropsychologist (Ashton, 2015) in the field of acquired brain injury. Ashton (2015) highlighted the key role of education in the child's development following a brain injury and argued that EPs' knowledge of the education system, pedagogical approaches and ability to work at different levels allows them to adopt the role of the "interpreter" between the fields of health and education.

The aim of this book is to address this imbalance by examining the relationship between the two disciplines from the perspective of EPs and with a focus on both their everyday practice and specialist role in child neuropsychology settings, with references to original research carried out by the author. The first chapter will consider the emergence of paediatric neuropsychology as a separate academic and practice discipline. In particular, the chapter will attempt to clarify child neuropsychology's distinct contribution compared to both adult neuropsychology and related fields such as neuroscience and neurology. Having defined and considered key conceptual issues linked to child neuropsychology, Chap. 2 will consider some of the more controversial aspects of the relationship between neuropsychology and education—an important context and key practice field for EPs. Specifically, the chapter will explore some of the most common neuromyths in education and will offer a critical examination of the appeal of overly simplified or misinterpreted neuroscientific findings, including the potential role of the EP in challenging those.

Following the broader contextual discussions presented in Chaps. 1 and 2, Chap. 3 will move on to focus on the applications of neuropsychology to EP practice by considering its relevance to both everyday EP practice and specialist neuropsychological casework. This discussion will be deepened further in Chap. 4, where the findings of the first national survey looking at EPs' views on neuropsychology will be presented and discussed. Chapter 5 will present perspectives from EPs working in specialist neuropsychological settings and healthcare professionals working alongside them, and will consider the specialist role of the EP in neuropsychology. Specifically, it will explore the motivating factors leading EPs to specialise in neuropsychology, their role and unique contribution to this specialist field, as well as common misconceptions about the role. Finally, Chap. 6 will present a discussion of the key issues that have emerged from the research findings and will explore the implications of those for the future relationship between the disciplines.

REFERENCES

Ashton, R. (2015). Educational neuropsychology. In J. Reed, K. Byard, & H. Fine (Eds.), *Neuropsychological rehabilitation of childhood brain injury: A practical guide* (pp. 237–253). London: Springer.

Ball, H., & Howe, J. (2013). How can educational psychologists support the reintegration of children with an acquired brain injury upon their return to school? *Educational Psychology in Practice, 29*(1), 69–78.

Bruer, J. T. (1997). Education and the brain: A bridge too far. *Educational Researcher, 26*(8), 4–16.

Gibbs, S. (Ed.). (2005). Neuropsychology [Special issue]. *Educational and Child Psychology, 22* (2).

Harrison, S., & Hood, J. (2008). Applications of neuropsychology in schools. In J. Reed (Revised J. Warner-Rogers) (Ed.), *Child neuropsychology: Concepts, theory and practice*, (pp. 404–420). Malden, MA: Blackwell.

Hood, J. (2003). Neuropsychological thinking within educational psychology. *DECP Debate, 105*, 8–12.

Mayer, R. E. (1998). Does the brain have a place in educational psychology? *Educational Psychology Review, 10*, 389–396.

Noble, T., & McGrath, H. (2008). The positive educational practices framework: A tool for facilitating the work of educational psychologists in promoting pupil wellbeing. *Educational and Child Psychology, 25*, 119–134.

Reed, J., & Warner-Rogers, J. (Eds.). (2009). *Child neuropsychology: Concepts, theory, and practice*. John Wiley & Sons.

Slomine, B., & Locascio, G. (2009). Cognitive rehabilitation for children with acquired brain injury. *Developmental Disabilities Research Reviews, 15*(2), 133–143.

Specialist Register of Clinical Neuropsychologists. (2020, January 29). Retrieved from https://www.bps.org.uk/lists/SRCN/search?refresh=1

Wilding, L., & Griffey, S. (2015). The strength-based approach to educational psychology practice: A critique from social constructionist and systemic perspectives. *Educational Psychology in Practice, 31*(1), 43–55.

CHAPTER 1

Child Neuropsychology as a Distinct Discipline

Abstract In order to explore neuropsychology's applications and relationship with educational psychology, it is important firstly to establish what is understood by the term "neuropsychology" and how it differs from the other neuro-disciplines. Specifically, this chapter will draw a distinction between neuroscience, neurology and neuropsychology and will highlight the ways in which the disciplines are similar and different in terms of their theoretical bases and focus. The second half of the chapter will explore the differences between adult and child neuropsychology, with a focus on why conclusions and frameworks from adult neuropsychology cannot always be applied to child neuropsychology.

Keywords Child neuropsychology • Neuroscience • Neurology • Adult neuropsychology • Brain development

Neuropsychology, Neuroscience or Neurology? Key Differences between the Neuro-Disciplines

Neuropsychology is commonly defined as the academic and practice discipline concerned with the relationship between brain structure, function and behaviour (Baron, 2010; Schoenberg & Scott, 2011, p. vii), with direct applications to a range of conditions in both adults and children such as, amongst others, developmental conditions, acquired brain injury,

© The Author(s), under exclusive license to Springer Nature Switzerland AG 2020
E. Misheva, *Child Neuropsychology in Practice*,
https://doi.org/10.1007/978-3-030-64930-2_1

epilepsy and dementia. Considering the broad definition and wide scope of neuropsychology as a subject and practice area, a number of related disciplines such as neurology and neuroscience may be perceived as having a similar focus and as overlapping with neuropsychology (Rose & Abi-Rached, 2013). As a result, the distinct contributions and differences between the main neuro-disciplines might not always be clear to practitioners in related fields, including psychologists. It is therefore important to explore and clarify how neuropsychology overlaps, relates to and differs from subject areas such as neuroscience and neurology.

While neuropsychology is a branch of psychology, neurology is a sub-specialty of medicine primarily concerned with the study and treatment of conditions arising as a result of damage or injury to the central nervous system, spinal cord or nerves (World Health Organization, 2016). Examples of neurological conditions include brain injuries, brain tumours, strokes, migraines, as well as congenital or degenerative disorders such as cerebral palsy, multiple sclerosis, Parkinson's disease, dementia and Alzheimer's disease (NHS England, 2018). Neurologists are physicians with specialist training in neurology who are involved in the assessment, diagnosis and treatment of conditions such as the ones listed above and are typically based in medical settings (Goetz, 2007). Neuropsychologists, in comparison, are primarily psychologists with postdoctoral specialist training in neuropsychology who may be based in a range of settings not necessarily restricted to the medical field, such as charities, rehabilitation centres and educational settings (Reed & Warner-Rogers, 2009).

While there is an overlap between neuropsychology and neurology in terms of the conditions they would typically encounter in their practice, the assessment and intervention approaches undertaken by neurologists and neuropsychologists are likely to differ significantly, given their distinct professional backgrounds in medicine and psychology respectively. More specifically, neuropsychologists may often be involved in the assessment, monitoring and intervention planning for a range of *neurological* conditions in children and adults such as epilepsy, degenerative conditions, brain tumours and injuries (Lezak, Howieson, Loring, & Fischer, 2012). However, their contribution to the understanding of the individual's needs is distinct from that of neurologists in a number of ways.

Neurological assessment, for example, is likely to focus on examining a range of primarily physiological and perceptual markers, such as the individual's reflexes, motor function, coordination, awareness and balance, as well as a number of sensation and perception abilities (eyesight, sense of smell, hearing, taste, swallowing and sensation in various body parts, (Goetz, 2007)). Neurologists may also use brain imaging (MRIs, CT scans) to further inform their assessment and diagnosis (Daroff, Jankovic, Mazziotta, & Pomeroy, 2015). Neuropsychological assessment, in contrast, will typically focus on the cognitive and behavioural manifestations of the condition (attention, memory, executive function, ability to solve complex problems), as well as on the possible emotional impact of the changes on the individual, through the use of psychometric assessment tools, as well as interviews and observational measures (Lezak et al., 2004). This, in turn, allows the neuropsychologist to obtain a profile of the individual's areas of strengths and difficulties, which will then inform their proposed interventions targeting the areas of difficulty (Reed & Warner-Rogers, 2009).

As such, neurological and neuropsychological approaches to assessment and intervention may identify distinct areas of need, as they focus on different aspects of brain and cognitive function. For example, an individual who has suffered a traumatic brain injury may present with a reduced attention span and executive function difficulties, as identified by a *neuropsychological* assessment, however their *neurological* assessment results may be unremarkable, with no identifiable difficulties with reflexes, general awareness or an impaired sense of smell or sight, for example. Similarly, a neurological assessment may identify that an individual has difficulties in an area such as balance, however the same individual may not have any identifiable neuropsychological difficulties. Thus, neurological and neuropsychological assessments and interventions have separate and distinct contributions and focus, and explore the presenting difficulties from two different angles, with the potential to identify different levels of need and remediation.

Finally, neuroscience, or the study of the function and structure of the nervous system and brain (Purves et al., 2018), informs yet is distinct from both neuropsychology and neurology. More specifically, neuroscience is an academic rather than a clinical practice area and it provides the theoretical foundations to disciplines such as neuropsychology. As outlined by Bear, Connors, and Paradiso (2007), neuroscience has a number of subdisciplines that study specific areas such as the link between brain and nervous system structure and cognitive function (cognitive neuroscience), the emergence of and changes occurring in the nervous system and brain over the course of development (developmental neuroscience) and how those processes relate to and affect the development of cognition over developmental time (developmental cognitive neuroscience).

Developmental cognitive neuroscience in particular provides a theoretical basis for child neuropsychology, highlighting the key role of *developmental change* in children's neurological and cognitive development (Johnson & de Haan, 2015). The implication of this for child neuropsychology practice and the distinction between paediatric and adult neuropsychology will be explored further in the next section.

Paediatric Neuropsychology and Adult Neuropsychology: Key Differences and Conceptual Issues

In order to consider paediatric neuropsychology's relevance to educational psychology practice, it is important to firstly explore how child and adult neuropsychology differ in their theoretical and practical approach. This subsection will review the evidence base of relevance to this question and will consider the implications of those differences for practice, and specifically for the educational psychology assessment process.

> "Child neuropsychology is the study of brain-behaviour relationships within the dynamic context of the developing brain." (Anderson, Northam, Hendy, & Wrennall, 2001, p. 3)

> "The process of change is key to child neuropsychology. This differs from adult neuropsychology, where the focus of study is on damage to an already developed brain." (Reed & Warner-Rogers, 2009)

Paediatric or child neuropsychology is a relatively young discipline in its own right, compared to the more established field of adult neuropsychology. Indeed, paediatric neuropsychology emerged as a separate field of study and practice informed by, yet independent from, adult neuropsychology relatively recently in the late twentieth century (Benton, 2000). Prior to that, adult neuropsychological models were highly influential and were applied to both adult and child populations. Adult neuropsychology, however, is primarily concerned with the changes to brain structure and cognitive function as a result of an injury or a condition that affects an already consolidated system, which in most cases had developed typically prior to the onset of the injury or condition. This highlights the significant challenges to the application of conclusions and frameworks used within adult neuropsychology to *child* populations; the changes observed in the context of an already consolidated system cannot be readily generalised and applied to the dynamic, constantly evolving context of the brain that is still developing in childhood.

The limits to the application of conclusions reached in the context of adult neuropsychology to child populations are particularly evident in the debate concerning whether domain-specific abilities are modularised independently (i.e. the view that abilities such as language, numerical reasoning and spatial orientation function independently from each other and that there are distinct modules in the brain to reflect this). For example, it is not uncommon for adult neuropsychology patients who have experienced brain injury to present with "deficits" in one specific area (e.g. language and reading), but to have seemingly intact abilities in other areas, such as face processing (Niogi et al., 2008; Young, Newcombe, Haan, Small, & Hay, 1993). This can be interpreted as evidence for the dissociation between these areas and as an indicator that, in this specific example, there are separate modules for language and face processing, completely independent from each other.

This had initially led some theorists in the field (commonly referred to as *nativists*) to suggest that the human brain is modularised from birth and that it is possible to talk about preserved and impaired modules in the case of developmental disorders and other similar conditions. For example, some theorists have claimed that in the case of Autistic Spectrum Conditions, the "theory of mind module" is impaired (Adams, 2011), presumably resulting in difficulties with social interaction and interpreting other people's emotional states. Research in the field of developmental cognitive neuroscience, however, has painted a more complex and nuanced picture of how cognitive function develops in children and how it is mapped and consolidated in the developing brain, thus highlighting key differences between adult and child neuropsychology.

Some researchers and theorists in the field have argued that the adult models provide a useful account of the "end-state" of development, however they are not suitable models for making sense of the "start-state" of development, as they fail to take into account the dynamic and complex process of developmental change and its impact on the developing brain and emergent cognitive functions (Karmiloff-Smith, 2009a; Farran & Karmiloff-Smith, 2012). More specifically, while few theorists and researchers would adopt an entirely empiricist perspective where the human brain is seen as a "blank slate" at birth, a more dynamic, neuroconstructivist conceptualisation suggests that "(…) the brain is a self-structuring, dynamically changing organ over developmental time as a function of multiple interactions at multiple levels" (Karmiloff-Smith, 2009a). Neuroconstructivism proposes that while some parts of the brain may have a bias towards processing certain types of input, different parts of the brain are not innately specialised to specific cognitive domains such as memory, language or reading (Westermann et al., 2007). Rather, it is suggested that, at birth, all areas of the brain are able to process a wide range and different types of information, however some areas are more relevant to the processing of specific types of input (Farran & Karmiloff-Smith, 2012).

From this perspective, the human brain is not static and modularised to begin with, albeit neuroconstructivists accept that there may be domain-relevant areas in the brain that are more suitable for processing certain types of input that become specialised gradually; rather, it is proposed that modularisation emerges over developmental time through a gradual process of specialisation, influenced by environmental input and stimulation (Westermann et al., 2007). Within this paradigm, the developing brain is seen as an interacting system where disturbance in one local area in the early stages of development can have a *cascading effect* on a range of cognitive domains at later stages (Karmiloff-Smith, 2009a, b), thus emphasising the importance of practitioners adopting a developmental approach to assessment and intervention. This may involve attempts to trace the child's developmental trajectory during the assessment process in order for the practitioner to be able to tailor any interventions more precisely, rather than come to a decision based on a "snapshot" of the child's presentation at a single point in time, which may no longer provide an accurate account of the area the child's present difficulties originated from (Farran & Karmiloff-Smith, 2012; Thomas, 2003).

Adult and child neuropsychology therefore emerge as related, yet distinct disciplines in terms of their underlying theoretical bases, as well as in terms of the assessment and intervention approaches that are best suited to them. While adult neuropsychology is most often concerned with changes to an already consolidated and modularised system, child neuropsychology focuses broadly on how brain-behaviour relationships emerge and develop over time, with a strong emphasis on the importance of developmental trajectories (Reed & Warner-Rogers, 2009).

REFERENCES

Adams, M. P. (2011). Modularity, theory of mind, and autism spectrum disorder. *Philosophy of Science, 78*(5), 763–773.

Anderson, V., Northam, E., Hendy, J., & Wrennall, J. (2001). *Developmental neuropsychology: A clinical approach*. Hove, UK: Psychology Press.

Baron, I. S. (2010). Maxims and a model for the practice of pediatric neuropsychology. In K. O. Yeates, M. D. Ris, H. G. Taylor, & B. F. Pennington (Eds.), *Pediatric neuropsychology: Research, theory, and practice* (2nd ed., pp. 473–498). New York, NY: The Guilford Press.

Bear, M. F., Connors, B. W., & Paradiso, M. A. (Eds.). (2007). *Neuroscience (Vol. 2)*. Lippincott Williams & Wilkins.

Benton, A. (2000). *Exploring the history of neuropsychology: Selected papers*. New York, NY: Oxford University Press.

Daroff, R. B., Jankovic, J., Mazziotta, J. C., & Pomeroy, S. L. (2015). *Bradley's neurology in clinical practice*. Elsevier Health Sciences.

Farran, E. K., & Karmiloff-Smith, A. (Eds.). (2012). *Neurodevelopmental disorders across the lifespan: A neuroconstructivist approach*. Oxford University Press.

Goetz, C. G. (Ed.). (2007). *Textbook of clinical neurology (Vol. 355)*. Elsevier Health Sciences.

Johnson, M., & de Haan, M. (2015). *Developmental cognitive neuroscience: An introduction*. Blackwell.

Karmiloff-Smith, A. (2009a). Nativism versus neuroconstructivism: Rethinking the study of developmental disorders. *Developmental Psychology, 45*(1), 56.

Karmiloff-Smith, A. (2009b). Preaching to the converted? From constructivism to neuroconstructivism. *Child Development Perspectives, 3*(2), 99–102.

Lezak, M. D., Howieson, D. B., Loring, D. W., & Fischer, J. S. (2004). *Neuropsychological assessment*. New York: Oxford University Press.

NHS England. (2018). Neurological conditions. Retrieved from: https://www.england.nhs.uk/ourwork/clinical-policy/ltc/our-work-on-long-term-conditions/neurological/

Niogi, S. N., Mukherjee, P., Ghajar, J., Johnson, C. E., Kolster, R., Lee, H., & McCandliss, B. D. (2008). Structural dissociation of attentional control and memory in adults with and without mild traumatic brain injury. *Brain, 131*(12), 3209–3221.

Purves, D., Augustine, G., Fitzpatrick, D., Hall, W., LaMantia, A., White, L., Mooney, R., & Platt, M. (2018). *Neuroscience*. Oxford: Oxford University Press.

Reed, J., & Warner-Rogers, J. (Eds.). (2009). *Child neuropsychology: Concepts, theory, and practice*. John Wiley & Sons.

Rose, N., & Abi-Rached, J. M. (2013). *Neuro: The new brain sciences and the management of the mind*. Princeton University Press.

Schoenberg, M. R., & Scott, J. G. (2011). *The little black book of neuropsychology: A syndrome-based approach*. New York: Springer.

Thomas, M. S. (2003). Multiple causality in developmental disorders: Methodological implications from computational modelling. *Developmental Science, 6*(5), 537–556.

Westermann, G., Mareschal, D., Johnson, M. H., Sirois, S., Spratling, M. W., & Thomas, M. S. (2007). Neuroconstructivism. *Developmental Science, 10*(1), 75–83.

World Health Organization. (2016). What are neurological disorders? Retrieved from https://www.who.int/news-room/q-a-detail/what-are-neurological-disorders

Young, A. W., Newcombe, F., Haan, E. H. D., Small, M., & Hay, D. C. (1993). Face perception after brain injury: Selective impairments affecting identity and expression. *Brain, 116*(4), 941–959.

CHAPTER 2

Neuromyths, Neurobabble and Pseudoscience: The Complex Relationship Between the Neuro-Disciplines and Education

Abstract Educational Psychologists' role is closely interlinked with the field of education. The relationship between the neuro-disciplines and education, however, is a complex and, at times, controversial one. This chapter will examine some of the reasons for this, beginning with a discussion of the possible factors behind the appeal of neuro-based information to educators and the general public. Next, an overview of some of the key neuromyths linked to education and learning will be presented, followed by a discussion of the prevalence of neuromyths in education and the possible role of the EP in challenging those.

Keywords Education • Neuromyths • Pseudoscience • Misconceptions

The previous chapter examined the differences between the neuro-disciplines and defined child neuropsychology in contrast to adult neuro-psychology, as well as neuroscience and neurology. The theoretical examination highlighted that the neuro-disciplines are complex fields and this complexity leads to high potential for misinterpretation by the media, general public and professionals who do not have sufficient background in them. The field of education is no exception to this. Indeed, the relationship between the neuro-disciplines and the broader field of education is a complicated and at times, a controversial one. As the role of the EP is closely associated with the education sector, Chap. 2 is going to explore this wider context and consider how misconceptions about the brain have become ingrained in the field and amongst educators.

BRAIN RESEARCH: SUBJECT OF FASCINATION AND DEBATE

The brain, its structure and function have captured the interest of both scientists and the general public for decades. The 1990s were famously declared "The Decade of the Brain" (Goldstein, 1994), reflecting the increased drive for brain-related research in the United States. Similarly, the twenty-first century has been deemed "The Century of the Brain" by some (Teramoto, Zuo, Zhang, & Kondo, 2015), with this narrative entering the wider public and political discourse in both Europe and the United States in the 2010s. During that period, a number of high-profile research projects linked to brain-related research were introduced, including the BRAIN Initiative announced by Barack Obama in 2013, as well as the European Union's "Human Brain Project", both of which aimed to advance our understanding of brain function and a range of brain and neurological disorders. A similar initiative with a specific focus on education was introduced in 1999 by the UK Centre for Economic Co-operation and Development (OECD). The OECD launched the Learning Sciences and Brain Research project with the aim of improving our understanding of cognitive neuroscience and its implications for learning and education. Thus, with the increasingly visible public profile of brain research, discussions linked to the neuro-disciplines and their wider implications were no longer restricted to university lecture halls, research centres or clinical settings. Instead, the links and applications of neuroscience in particular to fields such as psychology and education have become a topic of considerable interest (Dekker, Lee, Howard-Jones, & Jolles, 2012), but also intense debate.

While some have advocated for the important role neuroscientific findings can play in enhancing teaching and learning, others have expressed scepticism about the potential for direct application of neuroscience to education. On one side of the debate, Blakemore and Bunge (2012), amongst others, argued for the fundamental importance of neuroscience to education and stated that "to say that neuroscience is relevant to education is an understatement". They noted that, since the brain is implicated in all aspects of learning and it changes in response to newly acquired information, an improved understanding of how the brain processes information linked to learning is of great significance to education. In contrast,

Bruer (1997) described the relationship between the brain sciences and education as "a bridge too far" and noted that the appeal of brain sciences to educators, in combination with limited knowledge of this complex area, can lead to wrong interpretations of neuroscientific research.

Bruer (1997) was not alone in raising concerns about the potential for misinterpretation and overgeneralisation of neuroscientific findings and their applications to education. Indeed, his concerns have been repeated numerous times in recent years. For example, in 2002 the OECD high-lighted the high prevalence of *neuromyths*, defined by them as "misconception generated by a misunderstanding, a misreading or a misquoting of facts scientifically established (by brain research) to make a case for use of brain research in education and other contexts" (Organisation for Economic Co-operation and Development, 2002). Examples of neuromyths include, amongst others, the belief that people only use 10% of their brains, the notion of "the left and the right brain" and learning styles (Tokuhama-Espinosa, 2018, pp. 14–18). The issue of neuromyths in education was considered in additional detail by Howard-Jones (2014), who explored the factors that help neuromyths persist and concluded that they "flourish when cultural conditions protect them from scrutiny". In the next section, we are going to examine in more detail what some of these cultural conditions may be, followed by a critical exploration of key neuromyths in education and how they came about.

"Neurobabble" and the Intuitive Appeal of Neuro-Based Explanations

Neuromyths do not emerge and persist in a vacuum—their appeal cannot be easily separated from the broader appeal of the neuro-disciplines and brain research. Thus, in order to examine the factors that maintain them, we need firstly to explore what makes neuroscience and brain research so compelling to educators and the general public. Specifically, we will consider how *neurobabble*—neuroscientific information that is not relevant to an argument or explanation—has been shown to increase the credibility of an explanation in the eyes of neuroscience non-experts and the general public.

In their book *Neuroscience in Education: The Good, the Bad and the Ugly,* Della Sala and Anderson (2012) spoke about the "allure of everything "neuro" not just in the field of education, but on a broader societal level and in a range of areas such as economics, business, politics and marketing" (Della Sala & Anderson, 2012, p. 6). They argued that this appeal may be partially attributed to the seemingly more concrete brain-based explanations, compared to cognitive or psychological explanations of behaviours and phenomena, which may be perceived as more abstract and less "real". This perspective is supported by a well-known study carried out by McCabe and Castel (2008), which looked at how the inclusion of brain images affected people's judgement of the credibility and scientific reasoning of an accompanying article. Three experiments were carried out, where the participants were presented with a summary of a neuroscience research article, alongside either a brain image, bar graph, brain activation map or no image. The results indicated that the participants judged the article accompanied by a brain image to be more scientifically sound compared to the other options. Similarly to Della Sala and Anderson (2012), the authors argued that the images provide a seemingly concrete, physical basis for cognitive processes that are otherwise perceived as abstract, and thus give more credibility to the arguments and explanations given. Racine, Bar-Ilan, and Illes (2005) coined the term "neuro-realism" to describe this exact phenomenon—specifically, they noted that functional magnetic resonance imaging (fMRI) findings can be perceived as providing concrete, objective, physical proof for primarily experiential phenomena (i.e. experiences of pain or pleasure being validated as "real" by linking them to a specific brain area that "lights up" in an experiment).

However, interpreting fMRI scans is not a straightforward process for individuals with no prior training in the area, and it is easy to draw wrong or overly simplified conclusions about brain function based on wrongly interpreted fMRI research, as often seen in media reports. Racine, Bar-Ilan, and Illes (2006) carried out an analysis of how fMRI research is presented in print media outlets over a ten-year period and found that the majority of articles (67%) did not provide any technical details related to the fMRI scanning process, with a further 17% providing oversimplified explanations. This vagueness or lack of information can lead to misconceptions about what the process actually entails. For example, fMRI does not show neural activity directly; rather, it measures oxygenated blood flow. Thus, when fMRI images demonstrate that certain areas of the brain "light up" during specific tasks, this refers to the increased blood flow in response to the brain area being activated. Brain structures, however, are closely interlinked, and it cannot be readily assumed that no other brain areas apart from the one "lighting up" are implicated in the activity or process. Indeed, the notion that different skills or abilities are neatly positioned in distinct brain areas and those areas work in isolation is another example of oversimplification of neuroscientific information that leads to the development of neuromyths, such as the one purporting that academic skills are localised in distinct brain areas (i.e. a brain region for Maths/Music/Art), which we will examine in more detail in the next section.

Another landmark study provided further insight into the reasons why neuroscience has a "seductive allure" that fascinates the general public and gives more credibility to psychological explanations, even when the accompanying neuroscientific information is irrelevant to the argument. Weisberg, Keil, Goodstein, Rawson, and Gray (2008) presented non-expert adults, neuroscience students and neuroscience experts with descriptions of psychological phenomena, accompanied by one of four different kinds of explanations—"good" or "bad" explanations with a reference to neuroscience and "good" or "bad" explanations without a reference to neuroscience. The neuroscientific information referred to in the explanations *was not* of logical relevance to the explanations provided. The participants were then asked to rate how satisfying they found the explanations. While participants in all groups were able to differentiate between the good and the bad explanations irrespective of whether those were accompanied by neuroscience, the non-experts and neuroscience students judged "bad" explanations that were accompanied by neuroscience more positively. This suggests that the presence of irrelevant neuroscientific information seemingly gives more credibility to explanations the participants were otherwise able to discern as inadequate.

This phenomenon is also prevalent in education, where supposedly brain-based concepts and ideas are perceived as more convincing and credible by educators, even when the concept itself is not supported by research or is accompanied by *neurobabble*—neuroscientific information that is not relevant to the argument or explanation (Dekker et al., 2012; Della Sala & Anderson, 2012, pp. 3–6; Graham, 2013, p. 8). It is notable that the increased emphasis on evidence-based practice in disciplines such as education became more prominent in the 1990s (Davies, Nutley, & Smith, 2000; Hammersley, 2001; Trinder, 2000), and thus coincided with "The Decade of the Brain". It is therefore possible this has led to the false assumption that referring to supposedly "brain-based" learning strategies or concepts equals "evidence-based" practice or practice that is science-informed. However, by uncritically accepting the presumed superiority of brain-based explanations, including commercial for-profit "brain training" and learning enhancing programmes that claim to be based on brain research (Goswami, 2006; Graham, 2013), educators may also be more likely to accept common neuromyths as legitimate science simply because they contain references to the brain. In the next section, we are going to explore some of the key neuromyths linked to education and learning, as well as research into their prevalence and popularity amongst teachers.

NEUROMYTHS IN EDUCATION

The term "neuromyth" was originally coined by Alan Crockard, a neurosurgeon, in relation to the inaccurate ideas and understanding of brain function in medicine (Crockard, 1996). The definition was subsequently broadened by the OECD to include misconceptions about brain function based on misinterpreted, oversimplified or overgeneralised brain research findings that propagates their application to education and other contexts (Organisation for Economic Co-operation and Development, 2002). Many neuromyths are based on a distorted interpretation of an otherwise established scientific fact (Tokuhama-Espinosa, 2018, p. 12) and may seem to make "intuitive" sense. Neuromyths may therefore appear to be memorable and appealing, which, in turn, could increase their popularity and prevalence amongst both the general public and educational professionals. Below, we will consider some of the key neuromyths of relevance to education:

People Only Use 10% of Their Brain Power

The belief that people only use 10% of their brains is one of the most prevalent and persistent myths concerning brain function, which has also appeared repeatedly in the media and popular culture (Tokuhama-Espinosa, 2018, p. 23). For example, a number of recent Hollywood films have featured the 10% myth as their main premise—the 2014 film *Lucy* starring Scarlett Johansson used the tagline "The average person uses 10% of their brain capacity. Imagine what she could do with 100%," and the plot centres around the main character's newly unleashed abilities after she was able to access 100% of her brain power; similarly, the 2011 film *Limitless* was based on an almost identical premise, where the main character "unlocks" the full capacity of his brain with the help of a pill. The repeated references to the 10% myth in films and popular media have arguably solidified the general public's awareness and belief in it, regardless of the fact that there is no scientific evidence for it (Chudler, 2005). Indeed, the 10% myth has been identified as one of the most prevailing misconceptions about the brain amongst the general public (Hughes, Lyddy, & Lambe, 2013).

It is not clear where the 10% myth originated from, however there are a number of theories about its possible roots. Tokuhama-Espinosa (2018, pp. 23–24) noted that it may have originated from a misinterpreted quote by psychologist William James. In *The Energies of Men* James famously stated that "We are making use of only a small part of our possible mental and physical resources" (James, 1907, p. 323), which may have been interpreted to imply that people are not using their full brain power. Similarly, the 10% myth may have originated from the increased popularity of brain imaging research (Tokuhama-Espinosa, 2018, p. 23) and its reporting in the media; specifically, by demonstrating which parts of the brain "light up" while performing specific tasks, it may appear that no other brain areas or pathways are implicated. In reality, different brain areas and pathways are implicated in a range of tasks to varying degrees and brain imaging technology such as positron emission tomography (PET) and fMRI illustrate differences in brain activity, where the regions with the highest activity levels are clearly visible, whereas areas that have been activated to a lesser degree are not as visible, however this does not mean that they are not functioning. Indeed, as neurologist John Henley noted, individuals are likely to use 100% of their brains over the course of a day (as cited in Boyd, 2008). Similarly, Beyerstein (1999) pointed out that if most people used just 10% of their brain, then damage to the remaining 90% should not result in impairment or loss of abilities. This, however, is not supported by what we know from brain injury research, as injury to most areas of the brain will affect performance to varying degrees and periods of time, depending on the timing and severity of the injury (Crowe, Catroppa, Babl, Rosenfeld, & Anderson, 2012).

Learning Styles

Another highly prevalent and persistent myth in the field of education is the notion of learning styles. This myth implies that individuals have a predominant learning style (visual, auditory or kinaesthetic) and "brain-based" teaching in their preferred style enhances learning (Dekker et al., 2012). As is the case with many neuromyths, the learning styles myth originates from a legitimate scientific finding that has been misinterpreted or oversimplified. More specifically, while different types of information are indeed believed to be processed in different areas of the brain, the brain is also highly interconnected, with a substantial degree of communication between different regions (Dekker et al., 2012; Gilmore, McCarthy, & Spelke, 2007). It is therefore problematic and incorrect to suggest that information processing is restricted to a single sensory pathway. Indeed, while individuals may have a *preference* for a specific type of information, there is no evidence to suggest that restricting teaching input to a single sensory modality leads to improvements in learning (Lethaby & Harries, 2016; Riener & Willingham, 2010). Similarly, the validity of "learning styles" as a concept has been called into question. For example, Krätzig and Arbuthnott (2006) found that individuals' self-reported perception of their preferred learning style did not correspond to their learning style as identified by a questionnaire in more than 50% of cases. Similarly, no correlation was found between information presented in the preferred learning style and improved performance. This suggests that learning styles may represent an individual preference or bias, rather than reflect an actual biological or "hardwired" mechanism that would optimise an individual's capacity to process and retain information.

The learning styles myth has remained widespread amongst educators, despite compelling evidence against it and numerous attempts to dispel it. For example, one study found that over 88% of English language teachers believed that presenting information in the students' learning style enhances learning (Lethaby & Harries, 2016). This was consistent with the earlier findings of Dekker et al. (2012), who identified that the notion of learning styles was *the* most prevalent neuromyth amongst teachers, with over 80% of the sample indicating that they believe instruction in the students preferred learning styles leads to better learning. There are a number of possible reasons for the persistence of this specific myth. One potential fact could be found in the glorification of "brain-based" explanations, as discussed in the previous section; when combined with the push for evidence-based practice in teaching, the two concepts may be perceived as being equivalent and thus any concept labelled as brain-based may be regarded by some educators as being inherently scientific and contributing to evidence-informed practice. The widespread appeal of this specific myth highlights the need for neuro-literacy and a degree of criticality when considering supposedly brain-based concepts and explanations.

The Triune Brain Model: Do We Really Have a Lizard Brain?

Another example of oversimplified representation of brain function and evolution is the notion of the "triune brain". The concept was first introduced by Paul MacLean in the 1960s and was further developed in his book *The Triune Brain in Evolution* (MacLean, 1990). According to MacLean's theory, the human brain is organised hierarchically, in line with evolutionary processes, where humans have "inherited essentially three brains" (MacLean, 1964, p. 96).

According to MacLean, (1964), each of the three key regions, or brains, has with its own distinct function:

1. *The reptilian complex* (also referred to as the lizard brain/reptilian brain/primitive brain)—The reptilian complex or brain refers to the basal ganglia and was seen as the most primitive brain that evolved at an earlier evolutionary stage than the mammalian and late mammalian brain. It is primarily responsible for controlling basic impulses of key significance for survival, such as the fight-or-flight response, the ability to move and breathe, as well as sensations and instincts.

2. *The paleomammalian complex* (also referred to as the mammal brain)—The paleomammalian complex refers to the limbic system. According to MacLean's model, it evolved at a later evolutionary stage and is thus more complex than the reptilian brain. It is responsible for higher-order responses such as emotions and motivation.

3. *The neomammalian complex* (also referred to as the primate or human brain)—The neomammalian complex refers to the neocortex; this was seen as the youngest evolutionary addition to the brain present exclusively in higher mammals such as primates, as well as humans. It is responsible for more complex and sophisticated responses and functions that essentially make humans human, such as higher-order thinking skills, the ability to reason, think abstractly, plan and use language.

According to MacLean's model, over the course of evolution, the newer and more sophisticated brain structures were layered on top of older, less sophisticated ones, thus enabling the evolving animals to develop more complex behaviours and responses. This view, however, has been challenged by evolutionary biology, as neither species nor brain structures develop and evolve in a linear manner, as the model appears to imply (Cesario, Johnson, & Eisthen, 2020). More specifically, a very significant problem with the triune brain model, as identified by Cesario et al. (2020), is that it implies that evolution is a linear process where "primitive" or less complex organisms gradually evolve into more complex organisms, and thus gradually develop more complex brains than their predecessors (i.e. lizard→ rabbit → monkey → human). Evolution, however, is not a linear process—animals evolve from common ancestors rather than by gradually becoming a different, slightly more advanced species.

As is the case with many neuromyths, the triune brain model provides a seemingly intuitive and easy to understand explanation for complex phenomena such as brain-behaviour relationships. The concept has proved captivating for both academics and the general public alike. For example, scientist Carl Sagan referred to the triune brain in his popular book *The Dragons of Eden*, which is seen as having a key role in bringing the concept to the attention of the general public (Cesario et al., 2020). Similarly, despite the significant inaccuracies and oversimplification identified in the model, Cesario et al. (2020) note that it has since become a popular explanation of brain evolution in introductory psychology textbooks and in the field of psychology more broadly. Additionally, they highlight another problematic point related to the dichotomy implied by the notion of an animalistic, primitive brain that is responsible for impulsive decisions and the human, rational brain behind carefully considered decisions and actions. Specifically, they note that, in reality, other environmental or contextual factors are likely to have impacted on the organism or individual's decision making and ability to calculate risk and trade-offs. The authors give the example of the classic marshmallow experiments, where eating the marshmallow immediately may be perceived as a decision guided by the reptilian brain, rather than the rational human brain under the triune brain model. However, they point out that while waiting for a second marshmallow may be a worthwhile, adaptive response in a predictable and stable environment, eating the marshmallow immediately without waiting for a second one may be an equally adaptive and rational response if the context is otherwise uncertain and hard to predict:

impulsivity can be understood as an adaptive response to the contingencies present in an unstable environment rather than a moral failure in which animalistic drives overwhelm human rationality. (Cesario et al., 2020, p. 258)

Thus, a simple distinction between the primitive brain and its animalistic drives and the rational, measured decisions taken by the advanced human brain, as implied by the model, seems somewhat reductionist, in addition to the model's already questionable scientific foundations. Despite this, the appeal of the triune brain and metaphorical representations of the brain based on the model (e.g. Dan Siegel's "hand model of the brain") still persists. This can be attributed to their relative simplicity, but also their relevance to individuals' actual emotional experiences, where becoming angry, scared or startled may indeed feel like an almost animalistic reaction outside of one's conscious control. Similarly, Siegel's hand model of the brain can be seen as a useful metaphor for teaching children about emotional regulation; however, if the very foundations of the model are questionable and it does not, in fact, offer an accurate representation of brain function, the use of other established alternative models may be more appropriate. For example, cognitive behavioural approaches (Wyman et al., 2010), programmes that teach meta-cognitive skills (Davis, Levine, Lench, & Quas, 2010) or emotional coaching (Gus, Rose, & Gilbert, 2015) can be used to teach children emotional regulation and self-awareness, without the need to resort to using models that may inadvertently perpetuate myths or overly simplistic accounts of brain function.

Left Brain vs Right Brain

Another myth that implies the existence of distinct "brains within the brain" is the left and right brain dichotomy. This refers to the belief that the left and the right brain hemispheres have a separate, distinct role in learning, rather than being a unified system. Within this paradigm, the "left brain" is seen as being implicated in creativity, emotions and artistic activities, while the "right brain" is believed to be more logical, rational and scientific (Corballis, 2007, p. 291). The left brain/right brain myth can also be seen as related to the belief that certain academic skills are lateralised in specific brain areas (i.e. there is a brain region for maths, a brain region for music, a brain region for art).

However, as is the case with many other claims about brain function, the reality is not as simple and clear-cut as that. For example, language is considered to be one of the best examples of left hemisphere lateralisation as the two key areas implicated in language expression and production (the Broca and Wernicke's areas respectively) are positioned in the left hemisphere. Language, however, is a complex process that involves a number of different functions and skills (ability to distinguish between speech sounds, word retrieval, intonation, understanding of implicit meaning) and as is the case with other complex functions, many different brain networks are implicated in those processes. Tokuhama-Espinosa (2018) noted that word intonation and understanding sarcasm or humour are predominantly right-hemisphere lateralised. Similarly, Tokuhama-Espinosa uses the example of patient case studies where individuals living with half a brain following an injury are able to function and develop skills with undetectable differences compared to individuals who have both hemispheres; this suggests that while one hemisphere may be more dominant in terms of specific functions, those can be taken over by the other hemisphere in certain circumstances with minimal adverse effects (Tokuhama-Espinosa, 2018, p. 32).

This also highlights some of the challenges of associating specific brain areas with distinct academic skills. Similarly to language, and perhaps even more significantly, academic areas such as maths and reading are not simple, unitary processes; rather, they are the combination of a diverse range of different skills and competencies. More specifically, reading is the product of the combined input of a number of processes such as word recognition, eye movement control (Rayner & Pollatsek, 2013), recognition of semantic, orthographic and phonological word representations and text comprehension (Besner & Humphreys, 2012, pp. 1–2), as well as memory and attention. To argue that there is a distinct brain area for reading would imply that all of these processes are localised or restricted to the same area, networks and pathways, which is not the case. Indeed, the brain is highly interconnected and a large number of pathways are typically implicated in complex skills and processes such as learning and academic skills.

The Mozart Effect

The so-called Mozart effect refers to the now debunked belief that listening to classical music can boost students' intelligence and their performance on spatial tasks in particular. The misconception originated from a series of theoretical and research papers published in the 1990s (Rauscher,

Shaw, & Ky, 1993, 1995) which claimed that exposure to classical music, and Mozart in particular, enhanced students' performance on IQ tests. Despite the fact that the results have not been replicated by subsequent research (Pietschnig, Voracek, & Formann, 2010), the findings of the original studies were widely publicised and gained popularity amongst the general public, resulting in changes being introduced on policy level in at least two US states in the late 1990s. For example, in 1998, the US state of Georgia governor's proposed budget included separate funding to allow for classical music to be played to newborns in the state and, in the same year, Florida passed a bill introducing the play of classical music at children's centres (Pasquinelli, 2012; Tokuhama-Espinosa, 2018, p. 25). This highlights how seemingly harmless neuromyths or misconceptions can lead to very real implications and potentially affect thousands of people by redirecting funding and focus from other areas, as also pointed out by Tokuhama-Espinosa (2018, p. 25).

Similarly, the Mozart effect myth exemplifies two key issues related to the perception of neuroscientific or brain-based research. Firstly, as highlighted by some of the examples presented above, many neuromyths appear to provide a "quick fix" or a simple and straightforward-sounding explanation to an otherwise complex question, such as how can students be supported to learn more efficiently or can young children's cognitive development be enhanced by specific activities. By providing a seemingly brain-based explanation, those accounts may be perceived as more "real", "grounded in science" or "evidence-based" and their supposedly scientific basis can be used to justify interventions, as was the case with Mozart effect myth in some US states in the 1990s. This also highlights another, broader issue: while striving for evidence-based practice in education is undoubtedly important, if practitioners are not equipped with the skills to determine what constitutes good evidence and critically appraise information that may be grossly distorted in the media, neuromyths and pseudo-scientific concepts' appeal would likely persist in education.

How Prevalent Are Neuromyths in Education?

Research has consistently indicated that belief in neuromyths is highly prevalent amongst both trainee and qualified teachers, and this trend is observed worldwide, across countries and even continents, including in the UK (Howard-Jones, Franey, Mashmoushi, & Liao, 2009; Simmonds, 2014), the Netherlands (Dekker et al., 2012), Germany (Grospietsch & Mayer, 2019), the United States (Lethaby & Harries, 2016), Canada

(Macdonald, Germine, Anderson, Christodoulou, & McGrath, 2017), Brazil (Bartoszeck & Bartoszeck, 2012) and South America (Gleichgerrcht, Lira Luttges, Salvarezza, & Campos, 2015), Australia (Horvath, Donoghue, Horton, Lodge, & Hattie, 2018); Switzerland (Tardif, Doudin, & Meylan, 2015), Spain (Ferrero, Garaizar, & Vadillo, 2016), Greece (Deligiannidi & Howard-Jones, 2015; Papadatou-Pastou, Haliou, & Vlachos, 2017), Turkey (Karakus, Howard-Jones, & Jay, 2015), Portugal (Rato, Abreu, & Castro-Caldas, 2013) and China (Pei, Howard-Jones, Zhang, Liu, & Jin, 2015).

While there is a variability in terms of the types of neuromyths that are more prevalent in some countries compared to others, neuromyths are popular amongst teachers of all levels of experience, including both awarding-winning and non-awarding-winning teachers and regardless of level of interest in science and the brain (Grospietsch & Mayer, 2019). Indeed, some studies have suggested that teachers who report an interest in science are in fact *more* likely to believe in neuromyths and cannot easily distinguish between legitimate scientific findings and pseudoscience (Dekker et al., 2012). One possible explanation for this is that teachers with an interest in science and the brain may be using less reliable sources (i.e. the internet or television, rather than scientific journals) and may thus be exposed to wrong information more than those with no specific interest in science (Rato et al., 2013). Similarly, another explanation can be found in the so-called Dunning-Kruger effect—a bias where a limited amount of knowledge of a specific subject area can create the false belief that one knows more about the area than they actually do. Thus, it is possible that the educators who have an interest in science but limited knowledge acquired mainly through less formal sources are not aware of any "blind spots" they may have in their knowledge. This contrast is also highlighted by Grospietsch and Mayer (2019), who noted that "there seems to be a large gap between teachers' interest and their ability to actually deal with neuroscientific findings in a professional way".

One possible reason for the persistence of neuromyths in education was described by Lethaby and Harries (2016) as the "fundamental lack of communication between the fields of brain science and education" and the lack of opportunities for teachers to engage directly with neuroscientific research, rather than via secondary sources. Lethaby and Harries (2016) noted the role of teacher training in facilitating this process and used the example of Certificate in Teaching English to Speakers of Other Languages (CELTA)—the initial training course for teachers of English as a foreign language. They noted that "learning styles" was included as a topic in the official CELTA syllabus at the time of publication, meaning that teachers' practice could be assessed on the basis of whether they demonstrated awareness of learning styles while preparing for and delivering lessons. Others have also highlighted the role of initial teaching training in bridging this gap by providing teachers with some instruction around neuro-literacy during their training (Tardif et al., 2015; Papadatou-Pastou et al., 2017). However, while it may be tempting to attribute beliefs in neuromyths to ignorance or poor understanding of science that can be remediated quickly and easily by training in neuroscience, research in this field has painted a more nuanced picture. Specifically, research carried out by MacDonald et al. (2017) highlighted that training in neuroscience does not completely eliminate belief in neuromyths and many of those beliefs still persist even after exposure to neuroscience training. The authors highlighted that it is important that any courses or teaching on this topic is not restricted to passive instruction, but that it also incorporates "increased exposure to rigorous science" in the form of peer-reviewed journals as a way of challenging misconceptions (Macdonald et al., 2017).

Is There a Role for Educational Psychologists in Promoting Neuro-Literacy and Challenging Misconceptions About the Brain?

In light of Educational Psychologists' training as scientists-practitioners and regular contact with schools and teachers in their daily professional lives, it can be argued that, as a profession, EPs have a key role to play in promoting neuro-literacy amongst educators. However, it is important to acknowledge that EPs are not immune to belief in neuromyths and their training as EPs does not automatically suggest that they will be equipped to identify and challenge misconceptions about the brain. Indeed, up until 2006, it was a requirement for EPs to have trained as teachers prior to embarking on EP training and, given the high prevalence of neuromyths and misconceptions amongst the teacher population, it is possible that some EPs may not have been exposed to teaching disputing these misconceptions. Thus, as a first step in this process, EPs would need to examine their own beliefs and pre-conceptions about brain-based research, concepts and popular myths in order to be able to identify and challenge the misconceptions educators might have.

EPs may also have a key role in promoting neuro-literacy amongst educators, by highlighting the complexity of brain research and advocating for a cautious and responsible approach when referencing brain-related concepts. This may include modelling responsible use of brain references only when those are necessary, appropriate and based on evidence and sufficient knowledge of the evidence base and its strengths and limitations. However, this leads to an important question—how would EPs critically interpret findings from the neuro-disciplines if they do not have sufficient background knowledge in the field, or if they do not see this as part of their role? This is a key issue that we are going to consider in the next chapters, which will explore the relationship between neuropsychology and the practice of Educational Psychologists in more detail, with reference to both the existing literature and new research.

Further Reading

- Neuromyths: Debunking false ideas about the brain
  Tokuhama-Espinosa, T. (2018). *Neuromyths: Debunking false ideas about the brain*. WW Norton & Company.
- Your brain is not an onion
  Cesario, J., Johnson, D. J., & Eisthen, H. L. (2020). Your brain is not an onion with a tiny reptile inside. *Current Directions in Psychological Science*, 0963721420917687.
- The seductive allure of neuroscience explanations
  Weisberg, D. S., Keil, F. C., Goodstein, J., Rawson, E., & Gray, J. R. (2008). The seductive allure of neuroscience explanations. *Journal of Cognitive Neuroscience, 20*(3), 470–477.
- Neuroimaging: Many analyses, differing results
  Kayt Sukel, DANA foundation, https://dana.org/article/neuroimaging-many-analysts-differing-results/

References

Bartoszeck, A. B., & Bartoszeck, F. K. (2012). How in-service teachers perceive neuroscience as connected to education: An exploratory study. *European Journal of Educational Research, 1*(4), 301–319.

Besner, D., & Humphreys, G. W. (Eds.). (2012). *Basic processes in reading: Visual word recognition*. Routledge.

Beyerstein, B. (1999). Whence cometh the myth that we only use 10% of our brains? In S. D. Sala (Ed.), *Mind myths. Exploring popular assumptions about the mind and the brain*. John Wiley & Sons.

Blakemore, S. J., & Bunge, S. A. (2012). At the nexus of neuroscience and education. *Developmental Cognitive Neuroscience, 25*, 51–55.

Boyd, R. (2008). Do people only use 10 percent of their brains? *Scientific American*. Retrieved from https://www.scientificamerican.com/article/do-people-only-use-10-percent-of-their-brains/

Bruer, J. T. (1997). Education and the brain: A bridge too far. *Educational Researcher, 26*(8), 4–16.

Cesario, J., Johnson, D. J., & Eisthen, H. L. (2020). Your brain is not an onion with a tiny reptile inside. *Current Directions in Psychological Science*, 0963721420917687.

Chudler, E. H. (2005). *Do we use only 10% of our brain. Neuroscience for kids—10% of the brain myth*. Retrieved February 2, 2012, from http://faculty.washington.edu/chudler/tenper.html

Corballis, M. C. (2007). The dual-brain myth. In S. Della Sala (Ed.), *Tall tales on the brain* (pp. 291–313). Oxford: Oxford University Press.

Crockard, A. (1996). Confessions of a brain surgeon. *New Scientist, 2061*, 68.

Crowe, L. M., Catroppa, C., Babl, F. E., Rosenfeld, J. V., & Anderson, V. (2012). Timing of traumatic brain injury in childhood and intellectual outcome. *Journal of Pediatric Psychology, 37*(7), 745–754.

Davies, H. T. O., Nutley, S. M., & Smith, P. C. (Eds.). (2000). *What works? Evidence-based policy and practice in the public services*. Bristol: Policy Press.

Davis, E. L., Levine, L. J., Lench, H. C., & Quas, J. A. (2010). Metacognitive emotion regulation: Children's awareness that changing thoughts and goals can alleviate negative emotions. *Emotion, 10*(4), 498.

Dekker, S., Lee, N. C., Howard-Jones, P., & Jolles, J. (2012). Neuromyths in education: Prevalence and predictors of misconceptions among teachers. *Frontiers in Psychology, 3*, 429.

Deligiannidi, K., & Howard-Jones, P. A. (2015). The neuroscience literacy of teachers in Greece. *Procedia-Social and Behavioral Sciences, 174*, 3909–3915.

Della Sala, S., & Anderson, M. (Eds.). (2012). *Neuroscience in education: The good, the bad, and the ugly*. Oxford University Press.

Ferrero, M., Garaizar, P., & Vadillo, M. A. (2016). Neuromyths in education: Prevalence among Spanish teachers and an exploration of cross-cultural variation. *Frontiers in Human Neuroscience, 10*, 496.

Gilmore, C. K., McCarthy, S. E., & Spelke, E. S. (2007). Symbolic arithmetic knowledge without instruction. *Nature, 447*(7144), 589–591.

Gleichgerrcht, E., Lira Luttges, B., Salvarezza, F., & Campos, A. L. (2015). Educational neuromyths among teachers in Latin America. *Mind, Brain, and Education, 9*(3), 170–178.

Goldstein, M. (1994). Decade of the brain. An agenda for the nineties. *Western Journal of Medicine, 161*(3), 239.

Goswami, U. (2006). Neuroscience and education: From research to practice? *Nature Reviews Neuroscience, 7*, 406–413.

Graham, L. (2013). Neuromyths and Neurofacts: Information from cognitive neuroscience for classroom and learning support teachers. *Special Education, 22*(2), 7–20.

Grospietsch, F., & Mayer, J. (2019). Pre-service science teachers' neuroscience literacy: Neuromyths and a professional understanding of learning and memory. *Frontiers in Human Neuroscience, 13*, 20.

Gus, L., Rose, J., & Gilbert, L. (2015). Emotion coaching: A universal strategy for supporting and promoting sustainable emotional and behavioural well-being. *Educational & Child Psychology, 32*(1), 31–41.

Hammersley, M. (2001). *Some questions about evidence-based practice in education. Evidence-based practice in education.* Annual Conference of the British Educational Research Association, University of Leeds, England.

Horvath, J. C., Donoghue, G. M., Horton, A. J., Lodge, J. M., & Hattie, J. A. (2018). On the irrelevance of neuromyths to teacher effectiveness: Comparing neuroliteracy levels amongst award-winning and non-award winning teachers. *Frontiers in Psychology, 9*, 1666.

Howard-Jones, P. A. (2014). Neuroscience and education: Myths and messages. *Nature Reviews Neuroscience, 15*(12), 817–824.

Howard-Jones, P. A., Franey, L., Mashmoushi, R., & Liao, Y. C. (2009). The neuroscience literacy of trainee teachers. In *British Educational Research Association annual conference* (pp. 1–39). Manchester: University of Manchester.

Hughes, S., Lyddy, F., & Lambe, S. (2013). Misconceptions about psychological science: A review. *Psychology Learning & Teaching, 12*(1), 20–31.

James, W. (1907). The energies of men. *Science, 25*(635), 321–332.

Karakus, O., Howard-Jones, P. A., & Jay, T. (2015). Primary and secondary school teachers' knowledge and misconceptions about the brain in Turkey. *Procedia-Social and Behavioral Sciences, 174*, 1933–1940.

Krätzig, G. P., & Arbuthnott, K. D. (2006). Perceptual learning style and learning proficiency: A test of the hypothesis. *Journal of Educational Psychology, 98*(1), 238.

Lethaby, C., & Harries, P. (2016). Learning styles and teacher training: Are we perpetuating neuromyths? *ELT Journal, 70*(1), 16–27.

Macdonald, K., Germine, L., Anderson, A., Christodoulou, J., & McGrath, L. M. (2017). Dispelling the myth: Training in education or neuroscience decreases but does not eliminate beliefs in neuromyths. *Frontiers in Psychology, 8*, 1314.

MacLean, P. D. (1964). Man and his animal brains. *Modern Medicine, 32*, 95–106.

MacLean, P. D. (1990). *The triune brain in evolution: Role in paleocerebral functions.* Springer Science & Business Media.

McCabe, D. P., & Castel, A. D. (2008). Seeing is believing: The effect of brain images on judgments of scientific reasoning. *Cognition, 107*(1), 343–352.

Organisation for Economic Co-operation and Development. (2002). *Understanding the brain: Towards a new learning science.* OECD Publications.

Papadatou-Pastou, M., Haliou, E., & Vlachos, F. (2017). Brain knowledge and the prevalence of neuromyths among prospective teachers in Greece. *Frontiers in Psychology, 8*, 804.

Pasquinelli, E. (2012). Neuromyths: Why do they exist and persist? *Mind, Brain, and Education, 6*(2), 89–96.

Pei, X., Howard-Jones, P. A., Zhang, S., Liu, X., & Jin, Y. (2015). Teachers' understanding about the brain in East China. *Procedia-Social and Behavioral Sciences, 174*, 3681–3688.

Pietschnig, J., Voracek, M., & Formann, A. K. (2010). Mozart effect–Shmozart effect: A meta-analysis. *Intelligence, 38*(3), 314–323.

Racine, E., Bar-Ilan, O., & Illes, J. (2005). fMRI in the public eye. *Nature Reviews Neuroscience, 6*(2), 159–164.

Racine, E., Bar-Ilan, O., & Illes, J. (2006). Brain imaging: A decade of coverage in the print media. *Science Communication, 28*(1), 122–143.

Rato, J. R., Abreu, A. M., & Castro-Caldas, A. (2013). Neuromyths in education: What is fact and what is fiction for Portuguese teachers? *Educational Research, 55*(4), 441–453.

Rauscher, F. H., Shaw, G. L., & Ky, C. N. (1993). Music and spatial task performance. *Nature, 365*(6447), 611–611.

Rauscher, F. H., Shaw, G. L., & Ky, K. N. (1995). Listening to Mozart enhances spatial-temporal reasoning: Towards a neurophysiological basis. *Neuroscience Letters, 185*(1), 44–47.

Rayner, K., & Pollatsek, A. (2013). *Basic processes in reading.* In D. Reisberg (Ed.), *Oxford library of psychology. The Oxford handbook of cognitive psychology* (pp. 442–461). Oxford University Press. https://doi.org/10.1093/oxfordhb/9780195376746.013.0028

Riener, C., & Willingham, D. (2010). The myth of learning styles. *Change: The Magazine of Higher Learning, 42*(5), 32–35.

Simmonds, A. (2014). *How neuroscience is affecting education: Report of teacher and parent surveys.* Wellcome Trust.

Tardif, E., Doudin, P. A., & Meylan, N. (2015). Neuromyths among teachers and student teachers. *Mind, Brain, and Education, 9*(1), 50–59.

Teramoto, A., Zuo, H., Zhang, Y., & Kondo, T. (2015). The century of neuroscience. *Translational Neuroscience and Clinics, 1*(2), 73–74.

Tokuhama-Espinosa, T. (2018). *Neuromyths: Debunking false ideas about the brain.* WW Norton & Company.

Trinder, L. (Ed.). (2000). *Evidence-based practice: A critical appraisal.* Oxford: Blackwell Science.

Weisberg, D. S., Keil, F. C., Goodstein, J., Rawson, E., & Gray, J. R. (2008). The seductive allure of neuroscience explanations. *Journal of Cognitive Neuroscience, 20*(3), 470–477.

Wyman, P. A., Cross, W., Brown, C. H., Yu, Q., Tu, X., & Eberly, S. (2010). Intervention to strengthen emotional self-regulation in children with emerging mental health problems: Proximal impact on school behavior. *Journal of Abnormal Child Psychology, 38*(5), 707–720.

CHAPTER 3

Neuropsychology: A Specialism or a Fundamental Knowledge Base for All EPs?

Abstract This chapter explores an issue of central importance to the relationship between educational psychology and neuropsychology—does neuropsychology have applications to day-to-day EP practice, or is it primarily a specialist practice area? The first part of the chapter will focus on the possible applications of neuropsychological theory, and neuroconstructivism in particular, to everyday practice. The second part of the chapter will consider the existing literature on the contribution and role of EPs in casework involving neuropsychological conditions.

Keywords Child neuropsychology • Neuroconstructivism • Neurodevelopmental conditions • Educational psychologists • Epilepsy • Acquired brain injury

The previous two chapters have focused on examining the emergence of child neuropsychology as a distinct discipline and the sometimes problematic relationship between brain-based concepts and education. Chapter 3 will expand on this by focusing on the relationship between neuropsychology and the practice of Educational Psychologists. Specifically, in this chapter we will consider the possible applications of neuropsychology to generic educational psychology casework as well as specialist casework involving neuropsychological conditions, through the prism of the existing literature. This broader examination will serve as a foundation for the next two chapters, where we will explore those questions in more depth, from the perspective of Educational Psychologists themselves.

In the only paper published to date that explored the relationship between educational psychology and neuropsychology in a UK context, MacKay (2005) argued that the two subject areas have a "close and inter-dependent relationship", where "both draw from the academic foundations of mainstream psychology in its general and specialist applications, and the practice of each is informed by the approaches of the other". MacKay (2005) argued that neuropsychology need not be seen simply as a "bolt-on", highly specialist area that may be of interest to *some* EPs, but as an essential component of the wider knowledge base relevant to all EPs' practice. From this perspective, a simple distinction between neuropsychology as either a specialism or a discipline with broader applications to EP practice would be considered a false dichotomy. Indeed, as EPs work with a range of presentations and conditions of varying complexity, where often a range of cognitive, environmental and neurodevelopmental factors may be at play (British Psychological Society, 2018), it can be argued that a more holistic, neuropsychologically informed approach may provide more richness and specificity to psychologists' formulations and interventions (Hood, 2003). A more detailed exploration of how neuropsychology may be used to inform both EPs' day-to-day practice, as well as specialist work on neuropsychological cases, will be explored in more detail in the next subsections.

Neuropsychological Theory as a Fundamental Element of Educational Psychologists' Knowledge Base

Neuropsychology as a Potential Paradigm for Understanding Neurodevelopmental Conditions and Multiple Learning Needs

Some academics have argued that the applications of neuropsychological theory and concepts to the practice of psychologists working in educational settings need not be restricted to occasional specialist casework involving conditions traditionally associated with neuropsychology, such as, amongst others, traumatic brain injury, brain tumours or the epilepsies (Miller, 2009). While EPs may occasionally encounter cases of this nature, particularly in the context of special provision settings and Educational and Health Care Plan assessments, neuropsychology's relevance to cases in Educational Psychologists' day-to-day practice also needs to be considered. Indeed, if paediatric neuropsychology is defined as "the study of brain-behaviour relationships within the dynamic context of the developing brain" (Anderson, Northam, Hendy, & Wrennall, 2001), it can arguably provide a useful conceptual framework for a range of presentations and conditions EPs work with on a daily basis. Examples of those can be learning-related difficulties and neurodevelopmental conditions, where knowledge of brain-behaviour relationships can add another layer of understanding of the child's needs.

Annaz, Karmiloff-Smith, and Thomas (2008), for example, emphasised the importance of adopting a dynamic, developmental trajectory-focused approach to the study and assessment of needs of children with neurodevelopmental conditions of both known origin (e.g. Down syndrome, Williams syndrome) and of unknown or multivariate origin (Autistic Spectrum Conditions, dyslexia, dyspraxia). As EPs are likely to work with children presenting with difficulties of possible neurodevelopmental origin in their day-to-day practice such as the examples above (Educational Psychology, 2019), the more dynamic neuroconstructivist account of development can potentially provide them with a theoretical framework and an explanatory model of the complex presentations they may come across.

A specific example used by Farran and Karmiloff-Smith (2012) that illustrates why practitioners like EPs may wish to consider children's developmental trajectories, particularly in cases where a child may present with very pronounced difficulties in one area and with a seemingly "average" profile in others, is the case of children diagnosed with Williams syndrome. Williams syndrome is a genetic condition with a profile characterised by relatively strong language and social skills and more significant difficulties with visuospatial skills (Farran & Karmiloff-Smith, 2012). The seemingly uneven cognitive profile of children with Williams syndrome has been used by some nativists as evidence of the existence of different modules, independent of one another (Gerrans, 2003), as an impairment in one module (e.g. the module involved in visuospatial processing) does not affect other modules (e.g. the module responsible for language or social skills). However, a number of studies carried out with this population demonstrated that even in areas of relative strength, children with Williams syndrome used different mechanisms from typically developing children to achieve the same outcome (Hammond et al., 2005; Paterson, Girelli, Butterworth, & Karmiloff-Smith, 2006; Scerif et al., 2005). This suggests that areas of perceived relative strength are not necessarily "spared";

rather, the individual may have found another way of compensating for their difficulties in other domains that have also been affected in more or less subtle ways.

Therefore, from a neuroconstructivist perspective, it appears unlikely that a person will present with difficulties in just one isolated area (i.e. reading) without any more or less subtle implications for other areas of cognition or functioning. Rather, the reading-related needs are likely to have originated from a difficulty on a more specific local level, such as visual processing, which may have subsequently had a *cascading effect* on other areas throughout developmental time, where the reading difficulties may have emerged as the most pronounced manifestation of the local-level impairment. Some academics and researchers in the field have argued that it is therefore important that practitioners involved in the assessment and intervention process for children take into account their developmental trajectories in order to attempt to locate the underlying origin of the presenting difficulty (Karmiloff-Smith, 2009a; Annaz et al., 2008).

Additionally, Karmiloff-Smith argued that by grouping children in categories based on behavioural presentation alone, practitioners and researchers risk not taking into account the fact that those similar behavioural presentations might be the end result of different trajectories of atypical development that may also have had an effect on other areas of development, in less obvious ways. Thus, in the context of this paradigm, neuroconstructivists suggest that it is unlikely that atypical development would only affect one domain without more or less subtle implications for other areas. For example, Farran and Karmiloff-Smith (2012) argue that if an individual presents with what appears to be difficulty in the numeracy domain, with average scores in all other areas, this should not be interpreted as meaning that interventions should only target this domain. Instead, they argued that the practitioner would need to attempt to "trace back to infancy the origins of the number deficit, which might not be in the number domain directly; it could be a deficit in the visual system in the scanning arrays of objects." They elaborated that a difficulty in scanning may in turn have an impact on the function of other areas that rely on scanning proficiency to varying degrees. This can result in what may appear to be average performance in those domains; however, subtle difficulties may in fact be present but might not be immediately obvious.

This dynamic conceptualisation of cognitive and neural development can be seen as having significant implications for assessment and intervention planning in the case of EPs, as it offers an alternative framework that challenges the often static view of developmental conditions. Similarly, this model may also provide a partial explanation as to why some conditions commonly encountered in EP practice co-occur at rates much higher than would be expected by random chance. For example, dyslexia and dyspraxia have a comorbidity rate of between 60 and 70% (Iversen, Berg, Ellertsen, & Tønnessen, 2005; O'Hare & Khalid, 2002; Viholainen et al., 2006), approximately 40–45% of children diagnosed with dyspraxia would also meet the diagnostic criteria for Attention Deficit Hyperactivity Disorder (ADHD), Autism Spectrum Disorder (ASD) or dyslexia (Kaplan, Dewey, Crawford, & Wilson, 2001; Kaplan, Crawford, Cantell, Kooistra, & Dewey, 2006) and some studies have discovered comorbidity rates of 20–60% between dyscalculia and dyslexia (Dirks, Spyer, van Lieshout, & de Sonneville, 2008; Mayes & Calhoun, 2006).

Some researchers argue that it is therefore highly unlikely that the comorbidity between different neurodevelopmental conditions is just a coincidence. Gilger and Kaplan (2001), for example, suggested that developmental disorders are not necessarily the distinct, independent, "pure" conditions implied by diagnostic labels. They pointed out that, in fact, the evidence base suggests the opposite—"pure dyspraxia", "pure" developmental language disorder (DLD), "pure ADHD" or examples of cases where just one area of cognitive functioning is affected are very rare. It is important to note, however, that Gilger and Kaplan (2001) did not question the existence of reading, coordination, social communication and attention difficulties or the very real impact they have on individuals' lives. Rather, they argued that it might be more helpful for practitioners to conceptualise conditions of neurodevelopmental origin as a manifestation of an atypical pattern of development. The specific type of cognitive difficulty the individual presents with is in turn determined by the "timing, location and severity of the disruption in brain growth and development", meaning that some conditions may have shared risk factors.

Developing a coherent formulation that fully captures the child's needs from multiple perspectives is one of the fundamental aspects of the role of the Educational Psychologist (MacKay et al., 2016). As such, an understanding of the debates and alternative perspectives outlined above can arguably enhance EPs' formulations, thus highlighting the potential relevance and application of paediatric neuropsychology to educational psychology practice. It is important, however, to highlight, that the relevance of neuropsychology to practice disciplines such as educational psychology has been discussed in the literature mainly by academic psychologists, rather than practicing EPs. This raises a number of questions around the practical applications of any views and recommendations put forward in those papers. The original research presented in the next two chapters aims to address this imbalance, by directly exploring the views of EPs on the topic and thus attempts to bridge the gap resulting from the predominantly academic focus of this debate.

NEUROPSYCHOLOGY AS A SPECIALIST PRACTICE AREA

Educational Psychologists' Role and Involvement in Specialist Neuropsychological Casework

While the previous section has considered the possible wider applications and relevance of child neuropsychology theory to everyday EP practice, this section will explore the existing literature on the contribution and role of EPs in casework involving neuropsychological conditions. A significant proportion of children and young people with neurological conditions need ongoing monitoring and support with their changing emotional, social and educational needs (Walker & Wicks, 2012) and EPs are seen by some (Ball & Howe, 2013; Reilly & Fenton, 2013) as key stakeholders in the facilitation of this process. The added value and contribution EPs can make in those instances will be explored with a focus on two of the most commonly encountered neurological conditions in children—acquired brain injury and epilepsy.

Educational Psychologists' Role in Supporting Children with Acquired Brain Injury

Acquired brain injury is considered to be a leading cause of childhood disability, with potentially lifelong implications for the child's cognitive function, emotional wellbeing and academic learning (Forsyth & Kirkham, 2012). The term "acquired brain injury" refers to non-degenerative injuries or damage caused to the brain after birth (Headway, 2018; UKABIF, 2018), as opposed to congenital brain conditions such as microcephaly (small head circumference associated with smaller brain size) and some types of epilepsy that are present at birth. Acquired brain injuries can be divided into two broad categories—*traumatic brain injuries*, caused by damage to the brain as a result of an external force or injury due to falls, accidents or assaults (Headway, 2018), and *non-traumatic brain injuries*, typically caused by internal events such as infections (meningitis, encephalitis), hypoxia (oxygen deficiency), brain tumours, strokes and non-injury-caused brain haemorrhages (bleeding in or around the brain). The Glasgow Coma Scale is a tool commonly used to assess the severity of the injury on the basis of measuring consciousness through eye, verbal and motor response. Typically, a brain injury is likely to be classified as severe if the loss of consciousness lasted for over six hours, moderate where the individual was unconscious for between 15 minutes and two hours, and mild where the period of unconsciousness lasted for up to 15 minutes (Ball & Howe, 2013). The severity of the injury typically correlates with the range and seriousness of the symptoms experienced by the individual (Anderson, Spencer-Smith, & Wood, 2011).

The Kennard Principle of brain plasticity (Bennet et al., 2013) refers to the commonly held belief that "younger is better" when it comes to the age at which brain injury occurs, as children's brains can compensate for lost or impaired function in certain areas caused by brain injury better than adults. However, current research suggests that children are *not* in fact more likely to make quicker or better progress with their recovery following brain injury compared to adults (Anderson et al., 2011). Some researchers have argued that due to the fact that, in the case of younger children, the injury occurs in the dynamic context of a system that is still developing, where "early injury may compromise the development of neural networks underlying later stages of cognitive development" (McClusker, 2015, as cited in Ball & Howe, 2013), the child will "gradually grow into their symptoms" over developmental time (Brooks, Rose, Johnson, Andrews, & Gulamali, 2003). Indeed, research has suggested that younger children up to the age of eight who have experienced a traumatic brain injury have a wider range of long-term cognitive difficulties compared to older children and adults (Ball & Howe, 2013). More specifically, children under the age of eight have been found to have lower performance on a range of tasks measuring wider intellectual and visuospatial functioning compared to those who sustained a brain injury as adolescents (Verger et al., 2000). Similarly, younger children have been found to have more significant difficulties with language and overall worse intellectual functioning prognosis compared to adolescents (Fletcher et al., 1996). The implications of acquired brain injury occurring in childhood can therefore have profound implications for the child's cognitive, educational, behavioural and socio-emotional outcomes.

Walker and Wicks (2012) argue that acquired brain injuries are not the rare conditions that they are often perceived to be, with 1 in 500 children under the age of 16 experiencing a traumatic brain injury every year, thus making it likely that many educational settings, both mainstream and specialist, would encounter students who have experienced a brain injury. A small number of studies in recent years have looked specifically at the role of the EP in supporting children with similar neurological conditions. Ball & Howe, (2013), for example, looked specifically at the role of the Educational Psychologist in supporting children with brain injuries to reintegrate back to school. The study involved semi-structured interviews with a range of professionals working with children with acquired brain injury in two specialist settings.

A number of opportunities for involvement of EPs were identified, highlighting the unique role and contribution of EPs in the context of specialist neuropsychological cases. For example, the research identified that a specific contribution of EPs can make is to attend and contribute to initial discharge meetings, with the view of supporting the child's reintegration back to school where appropriate, as well as to help school staff make sense of the medical and neurological information outlined in reports and what it means in practical terms for the child's ability to engage in learning. Ball and Howe (2013) highlighted that "often it is the educational psychology service that remains involved with the child through their school life and therefore is a key agency to communicate information about the injury to future settings".

Similarly, as education is regarded as a fundamental part of the child's recovery (Slomine & Locascio, 2009), providing school staff with appropriate training and guidance in relation to the child's changing psychological and cognitive needs, rather than just their physical needs, was seen as fundamental to the child's successful reintegration and ongoing support they can access in their educational setting. EPs were seen as having a key role in providing training and support to school staff, with a focus on highlighting the ongoing and changing needs of this population and reminding staff that the child's presentation may not be static or follow a linear path to recovery.

These two potential roles for EPs in specialist casework involving acquired brain injuries raised a number of questions of the training needs of Educational Psychologists themselves, as the initial EP training may not have equipped them with the knowledge and skills in this area required to support the children and staff in this context (Bozic & Morris, 2005). Indeed, Ball and Howe (2013) recommended, based on their research findings, that all initial training courses in Educational Psychology should have a module on brain injury and neuropsychological development, as well as that Educational Psychology Services should ensure that they have practitioners with some specialist knowledge in the areas of neuropsychology and brain injury. It is not, however, possible to establish whether these recommendations have been taken into consideration or implemented on a larger scale, as no subsequent research has examined this specific issue. Similarly, there is currently no centralised way of collecting data on how individual services address the needs of children with neurological and neuropsychological conditions such as acquired brain injury, thus highlighting the need for more research looking at this specific area of practice.

Finally, it is important to take into consideration the fact that research looking at the role of EPs in neuropsychological cases is still in its infancy, and the existing studies are typically small in scale. While this does not necessarily preclude the generalisability and validity of the findings, it is important to interpret them cautiously, with due consideration for their limitations. Ball and Howe's (2013) paper, for example, was based on interviews with eight participants from a range of professional backgrounds. While no detailed breakdown of the exact number of participants from each profession was included, the small, yet non-homogenous sample raises the possibility that the findings were more reflective of the individual practitioner's views, with limited scope for generalisation. Similarly, the interviews were conducted in two specialist settings, and given that provision and practices may vary from one service to another, this raises questions as to whether the study's conclusions and recommendations would be applicable on a larger scale, or if they are specific to the two specialist settings. However, this does not suggest that Ball and Howe's findings are not informative of the potential role of EPs in cases of acquired brain injury, despite their limitations. The study arguably provides an account of some of the possible ways in which EPs can contribute to the care of children with acquired brain injury, and this initial account can subsequently serve as a foundation for larger-scale research.

Educational Psychologists' Role in Supporting Children with Epilepsy
Similarly to childhood acquired brain injury, epilepsy is one of the most commonly encountered conditions of neurological origin in children. Indeed, epilepsy has consistently been found to be *the most common* chronic childhood neurological condition (Aaberg et al., 2017; Bell et al., 2014; Reilly & Fenton, 2013), with prevalence rates of between 0.5 and 1% of the total child population, similar to the prevalence rates of Autistic Spectrum Conditions. This suggests that, on average, 1 out of 150 children will be diagnosed with epilepsy (Aaberg et al., 2017; Epilepsy Action, 2018), meaning that every primary school is likely to have at least one pupil diagnosed with the condition.

Epilepsy is characterised by a range of recurrent seizures caused by a disturbance in the electrical signals sent between neurons (Epilepsy Society, 2018a). The resulting atypical or excessive pattern of electrical activity can lead to different types of epileptic seizures that can affect the entire brain in the case of generalised seizures, or a specific area of the brain, in the case of focal seizures (Reilly & Fenton, 2013). Different types of seizures are characterised by different physical manifestations such as the person becoming unresponsive (absence seizures), jerking bodily movements (clonic seizures) or sudden onset of body muscle stiffness (tonic seizures). Epileptic seizures can be caused by genetic factors and predispositions and may emerge in early childhood; however, they can also be caused by external factors such as infections like meningitis, or following a stroke or a head injury (Epilepsy Society, 2018b).

The extent to which epilepsy will affect individual children's social, emotional and educational functioning varies significantly (Jensen, 2011), depending on the type and severity of the condition, seizures and treatment. However, the association between epilepsy, education and learning-related difficulties is well-documented, with 20–30% of children with epilepsy having learning disabilities (Berg, 2011), 48% having a specific learning difficulty (Fastenau, Shen, Dunn, & Austin, 2008) and 35% of children with epilepsy in the UK having a statement of special educational needs, now known as Educational and Health Care Plan (Swiderske, Gondwe, Joseph, & Gibbs, 2011). Similarly, children with epilepsy are more likely to be diagnosed with Attention Deficit Hyperactivity disorder (ADHD), and the inattentive subtype specifically, with rates of 12%–21% (Swiderske et al., 2011). Those affected may therefore require ongoing support and adaptations in terms of their learning, physical and emotional needs and EPs can have a key role in the identification and coordinated response to those needs from a psychological perspective.

Reilly and Fenton (2013) looked specifically at the possible role and contribution of EPs in supporting children diagnosed with epilepsy. They identified a number of potential areas for EP involvement at both the individual and the systemic level. More specifically, a number of studies have highlighted the lack of knowledge of epilepsy and its possible implications for learning that teachers experience, meaning that they are often reliant on the child's parents for advice and information (Wodrich, Jarrar, Buchhalter, Levy, & Gay, 2011). Similarly, both parents and teachers may become overprotective of the child, resulting in lowered expectations in the case of teachers (Prpic et al., 2003), or keeping the child off school, in the case of parents (Wodrich & Cunningham, 2008). EPs may therefore have a key role in supporting teachers to develop their understanding of the specific type of epilepsy the child experiences, as well as their profile of strengths and difficulties and how those may manifest themselves in the classroom, as well as socially.

Similarly, Reilly and Fenton (2013) suggest that EPs, alongside medical professionals, can support education staff by helping them distinguish between the needs of the child that may be of medical origin, and those that may best respond to educational or psychological input. In the case of parents, the role of the EP may involve providing parents with support around managing behaviour and boundaries at home, as well as with support around the parent's understanding of the child's cognitive and learning needs and how those may impact on their wider functioning. Reilly and Fenton (2013) point out, however, that in order to be able to do this, psychologists "will need a sound understanding of the variables that contribute to cognitive and behavioural issues in childhood epilepsy". This appears to mirror the points raised by Ball and Howe (2013) in relation to the role of EPs in cases of acquired brain injury, as outlined in the previous section, where the importance of developing EPs' understanding of neurological development and brain injury was a key recommendation.

While a number of studies have looked at the role and contribution of Educational Psychologists in cases involving specific neurological conditions, the current understanding of the broader role of EPs working in neuropsychological settings is very limited. Albeit informative about their respective topics, the existing empirical papers in this subject and practice areas are small in number and scale. While they have all indicated that there are a number of potential roles for EPs to contribute to cases of neurological nature, the evidence base has not yet developed sufficiently to provide further insights about these possible roles in practice. This highlights the need for further research in this area, with a focus on initially identifying general trends and practices in relation to EPs' work and involvement with a broad range of childhood neurological conditions.

Chapter 4 will aim to provide some answers to those questions with reference to the first national survey that systematically explored the views, attitudes and perceptions EPs hold about neuropsychology, including the perceived relevance and applications of neuropsychology theory and research on day-to-day EP practice, as well as the most commonly encountered neurological conditions in day-to-day EP practice.

Further Reading

- Are neurodevelopmental disorders discrete conditions?
  Misheva, E. (2018). *Are neurodevelopmental disorders discrete conditions?* https://thepsychologist.bps.org.uk/volume-31/august-2018/are-neurodevelopmental-disorders-discrete-conditions
- The importance of tracing developmental trajectories
  Annaz, D., Karmiloff-Smith, A., & Thomas, M. S. (2008). The importance of tracing developmental trajectories for clinical child neuropsychology. In J. Reed & J. Warner-Rogers (Eds.), *Child neuropsychology: Concepts, theory and practice* (pp. 7–18). Hoboken: Wiley Blackwell.
- Neuroconstructivism: How the brain constructs cognition
  Mareschal, D., Johnson, M. H., Sirois, S., Thomas, M. S., Spratling, M., & Westermann, G. (2007). *Neuroconstructivism: How the brain constructs cognition* (Vol. 1). Oxford University Press.
  Mareschal, D., Sirois, S., Johnson, M. H., & Westermann, G. (2007). *Neuroconstructivism: perspectives and prospects (Vol. 2).* Oxford University Press.
- What's in a name?
  Bishop, D. (2010, 18 December). What's in a name? [Blog post]. BishopBlog. Retrieved 10 April 2018 from http://deevybee.blogspot.co.uk/2010/12/whats-in-name.html
- Neurodevelopmental disorders across the lifespan: A neuroconstructivist approach
  Farran, E. K., & Karmiloff-Smith, A. (Eds.). (2012). *Neurodevelopmental disorders across the lifespan: A neuroconstructivist approach.* Oxford University Press.
- Educational Neuropsychology
  Ashton, R. (2015). Educational neuropsychology. In Reed, J., Byard, K., & Fine, H. (Eds.). *Neuropsychological rehabilitation of childhood brain injury: A practical guide.* (pp. 237–253). London: Springer.

References

Aaberg, K. M., Gunnes, N., Bakken, I. J., Søraas, C. L., Berntsen, A., Magnus, P., & Surén, P. (2017). Incidence and prevalence of childhood epilepsy: A nationwide cohort study. *Pediatrics,* e20163908.

Anderson, V., Northam, E., Hendy, J., & Wrennall, J. (2001). *Developmental neuropsychology: A clinical approach*. Hove, UK: Psychology Press.

Anderson, V., Spencer-Smith, M., & Wood, A. (2011). Do children really recover better? Neurobehavioural plasticity after early brain insult. *Brain, 134*(8), 2197–2221.

Annaz, D., Karmiloff-Smith, A., & Thomas, M. S. (2008). The importance of tracing developmental trajectories for clinical child neuropsychology. In J. Reed & J. Warner-Rogers (Eds.), *Child neuropsychology: Concepts, theory and practice* (pp. 7–18). Hoboken: Wiley Blackwell.

Ball, H., & Howe, J. (2013). How can educational psychologists support the reintegration of children with an acquired brain injury upon their return to school? *Educational Psychology in Practice, 29*(1), 69–78.

Bell, G. S., Neligan, A., & Sander, J. W. (2014). An unknown quantity—The worldwide prevalence of epilepsy. *Epilepsia, 55*(7), 958–962.

Bennet, L., Van Den Heuij, L. M., Dean, J., Drury, P., Wassink, G., & Jan Gunn, A. (2013). Neural plasticity and the Kennard principle: Does it work for the preterm brain? *Clinical and Experimental Pharmacology and Physiology, 40*(11), 774–784.

Berg, A. T. (2011). Epilepsy, cognition, and behavior: The clinical picture. *Epilepsia, 52*, 7–12.

Bozic, N., & Morris, S. (2005). Traumatic brain injury in childhood and adolescence: The role of educational psychology services in promoting effective recovery. *Educational and Child Psychology, 22*(2), 108–120.

British Psychological Society. (2018). *Careers in educational psychology*. Retrieved November 14, 2018, from https://careers.bps.org.uk/area/educational

Brooks, B. M., Rose, F. D., Johnson, D. A., Andrews, T. K., & Gulamali, R. (2003). Support for children following traumatic brain injury: The views of educational psychologists. *Disability and Rehabilitation, 25*(1), 51–56.

Dirks, E., Spyer, G., van Lieshout, E. C., & de Sonneville, L. (2008). Prevalence of combined reading and arithmetic disabilities. *Journal of Learning Disabilities, 41*, 460–473.

Educational Psychology. (2019, April 10). *Educational Psychology*. Retrieved from https://careers.bps.org.uk/area/educational

Epilepsy Action. (2018). Epilepsy facts. Retrieved from https://www.epilepsy.org.uk/press/facts

Epilepsy Society. (2018a). Why do seizures happen?. Retrieved from https://www.epilepsysociety.org.uk/why-do-seizures-happen#.XC0ofmj7SgB

Epilepsy Society. (2018b). Seizure types. Retrieved from https://www.epilepsysociety.org.uk/seizure-types#.XC0oeWj7SgB

Farran, E. K., & Karmiloff-Smith, A. (Eds.). (2012). *Neurodevelopmental disorders across the lifespan: A neuroconstructivist approach*. Oxford University Press.

Fastenau, P. S., Shen, J., Dunn, D. W., & Austin, J. K. (2008). Academic under-achievement among children with epilepsy: Proportion exceeding psychometric criteria for learning disability and associated risk factors. *Journal of Learning Disabilities, 41*(3), 195–207.

Fletcher, J. M., Levin, H. S., Lachar, D., Kusnerik, L., Harward, H., Mendelsohn, D., & Lilly, M. A. (1996). Behavioral outcomes after pediatric closed head injury: Relationships with age, severity, and lesion size. *Journal of Child Neurology, 11*(4), 283–290.

Forsyth, R., & Kirkham, F. (2012). Predicting outcome after childhood brain injury. *Canadian Medical Association Journal, 184*(11), 1257–1264.

Gerrans, P. (2003). Nativism and neuroconstructivism in the explanation of Williams syndrome. *Biology and Philosophy, 18*(1), 41–52.

Gilger, J. W., & Kaplan, B. J. (2001). Atypical brain development: A conceptual framework for understanding developmental learning disabilities. *Developmental Neuropsychology, 20*(2), 465–481.

Hammond, P., Hutton, T. J., Allanson, J. E., Buxton, B., Campbell, L. E., Clayton-Smith, J., et al. (2005). Discriminating power of localized three-dimensional facial morphology. *The American Journal of Human Genetics, 77*(6), 999–1010.

Headway. (2018). Types of brain injury. Retrieved from https://www.headway.org.uk/about-brain-injury/individuals/types-of-brain-injury/

Hood, J. (2003). Neuropsychological thinking within educational psychology. *DECP Debate, 105*, 8–12.

Iversen, S., Berg, K., Ellertsen, B., & Tønnessen, F. E. (2005). Motor coordination difficulties in a municipality group and in a clinical sample of poor readers. *Dyslexia, 11*(3), 217–231.

Jensen, F. E. (2011). Epilepsy as a spectrum disorder: Implications from novel clinical and basic neuroscience. *Epilepsia, 52*, 1–6.

Kaplan, B. J., Dewey, D. M., Crawford, S. G., & Wilson, B. N. (2001). The term comorbidity is of questionable value in reference to developmental disorders: Data and theory. *Journal of Learning Disabilities, 34*(6), 555–565.

Kaplan, B., Crawford, S., Cantell, M., Kooistra, L., & Dewey, D. (2006). Comorbidity, co-occurrence, continuum: What's in a name? *Child: Care, Health and Development, 32*(6), 723–731.

Karmiloff-Smith, A. (2009a). Nativism versus neuroconstructivism: Rethinking the study of developmental disorders. *Developmental Psychology, 45*(1), 56.

MacKay, T. (2005). The relationship of educational psychology and clinical neuropsychology. *Educational and Child Psychology, 22*(2), 7–17.

MacKay, T., Lauchlan, F., Lindsay, G., Monsen, J., Frederickson, N., Gameson, J., & Rees, I. (2016). *Frameworks for practice in educational psychology: A textbook for trainees and practitioners.* Jessica Kingsley Publishers.

Mayes, S. D., & Calhoun, S. L. (2006). Frequency of reading, math and writing disabilities in children with clinical disorders. *Learning and Individual Differences, 16*, 145–157.

Miller, D. C. (Ed.). (2009). *Best practices in school neuropsychology: Guidelines for effective practice, assessment, and evidence-based intervention.* John Wiley & Sons.

O'Hare, A., & Khalid, S. (2002). The association of abnormal cerebellar function in children with developmental coordination disorder and reading difficulties. *Dyslexia, 8*(4), 234–248.

Paterson, S. J., Girelli, L., Butterworth, B., & Karmiloff-Smith, A. (2006). Are numerical impairments syndrome specific? Evidence from Williams syndrome and Down's syndrome. *Journal of Child Psychology and Psychiatry, 47*(2), 190–204.

Prpic, I., Korotaj, Z., Vlašic-Cicvaric, I., Paucic-Kirincic, E., Valerjev, A., & Tomac, V. (2003). Teachers' opinions about capabilities and behavior of children with epilepsy. *Epilepsy & Behavior, 4*(2), 142–145.

Reilly, C., & Fenton, V. (2013). Children with epilepsy: The role of the educational psychologist. *Educational Psychology in Practice, 29*(2), 138–151.

Scerif, G., Karmiloff-Smith, A., Campos, R., Elsabbagh, M., Driver, J., & Cornish, K. (2005). To look or not to look? Typical and atypical development of oculomotor control. *Journal of Cognitive Neuroscience, 17*(4), 591–604.

Slomine, B., & Locascio, G. (2009). Cognitive rehabilitation for children with acquired brain injury. *Developmental Disabilities Research Reviews, 15*(2), 133–143.

Swiderske, N., Gondwe, J., Joseph, J., & Gibbs, J. (2011). The prevalence and management of epilepsy in secondary school pupils with and without special educational needs. *Child: Care Health and Development, 37,* 96–102.

UKABIF. (2018). About brain injury. Retrieved from https://www.ukabif.org.uk/about-brain-injury/

Verger, K., Junqué, C., Jurado, M. Á., Tresserras, P., Bartumeus, F., Nogues, P., & Poch, J. M. (2000). Age effects on long-term neuropsychological outcome in paediatric traumatic brain injury. *Brain Injury, 14*(6), 495–503.

Viholainen, H., Ahonen, T., Lyytinen, P., Cantell, M., Tolvanen, A., & Lyytinen, H. (2006). Early motor development and later language and reading skills in children at risk of familial dyslexia. *Developmental Medicine and Child Neurology, 48*(5), 367–373.

Walker, S., & Wicks, B. (2012). *Educating children and young people with acquired brain injury.* Routledge.

Wodrich, D. L., & Cunningham, M. M. (2008). School-based tertiary and targeted interventions for students with chronic medical conditions: Examples from type 1 diabetes mellitus and epilepsy. *Psychology in the Schools, 45*(1), 52–62.

Wodrich, D. L., Jarrar, R., Buchhalter, J., Levy, R., & Gay, C. (2011). Knowledge about epilepsy and confidence in instructing students with epilepsy: Teachers' responses to a new scale. *Epilepsy & Behavior, 20*(2), 360–365.

CHAPTER 4

Child Neuropsychology's Application to Practice: Perspectives from Eps

Abstract The EP perspective is distinctly missing from the neuropsychology academic and research literature, resulting in a significant knowledge gap regarding the relationship between the two disciplines. In an attempt to fill this gap, this chapter will explore Educational Psychologists' attitudes towards child neuropsychology, its applications to day-to-day practice as well as EPs' familiarity with neuropsychology as a specialism available to them. These key questions will be considered in the context of the findings of the first national survey exploring EPs' views on neuropsychology in the UK.

Keywords Training • Paediatric neuropsychology • Neurological conditions • National survey

THE NATIONAL SURVEY: AN OVERVIEW

The national survey was carried out by the author between February and April 2019 and the sample consisted of 200 trainee and qualified EPs. The biggest respondent group were maingrade EPs (50% of the sample), followed by trainee EPs (28%), senior or principal EPs (16%), EPs in private practice (5%) and EPs in specialist posts (3%). The survey consisted of a series of open- and close-ended questions related to EPs' attitudes towards neuropsychology, including its perceived relevance and applications to

© The Author(s), under exclusive license to Springer Nature Switzerland AG 2020
E. Misheva, *Child Neuropsychology in Practice*,
https://doi.org/10.1007/978-3-030-64930-2_4

day-to-day EP practice, experiences of working with neuropsychological conditions and familiarity with neuropsychology as a specialism option.

A number of steps were undertaken to ensure that the participant distribution across the country reflected that national distribution of EPs in the UK by region. All participants were asked to declare whether they were a qualified or trainee EP in the UK, and to indicate the geographical region they were based in, in order to ensure that the sample consisted of UK-based EPs/TEPs. As no records detailing the number of EPs employed in each region of the country are publicly available, a request was made under the Freedom of Information Act to the Health and Care Professions Council (HCPC)—the regulatory body for practitioner psychologists, requesting this information. Once the national data were obtained, they were cross-referenced with the distribution of participants in the sample and four regions were found to be particularly underrepresented (Scotland, Norfolk, the South West and Northern Ireland). Educational Psychology Services in those geographical areas were approached directly, thus increasing the representation of these regions in the data.

We will consider the national survey's findings below, in the context of three key areas—EPs' perceptions of and attitudes towards child neuropsychology, the relevance of child neuropsychology to everyday EP practice and the way in which EPs apply neuropsychology-related knowledge in their practice.

EPs' Perceptions of and Attitudes Towards Child Neuropsychology as an Academic and Practice Discipline

Do EPs Refer to Child Neuropsychology Theory in Their Day-to-Day Practice?

The majority of the respondents to the national survey reported that they used neuropsychological concepts in their daily practice and saw neuropsychology as relevant to EP practice. However, while over 70% stated that they referred to neuropsychology in their work, their self-reported understanding of what neuropsychological theory and practice entail was significantly lower, with less than 25% reporting having a good or high level of knowledge. Even more significantly, just 18% of EPs said they were familiar or very familiar with the distinction between neuroscience and neuropsychology. This raises an important question regarding the use of neuropsychology concepts in EP practice—if the majority of EPs report that they are not confident about their knowledge and understanding of neuropsychology and cannot identify how neuropsychology is different from neuroscience, it is not clear whether they would be able to accurately identify neuropsychological concepts and distinguish them from neuroscientific concepts, for example. Therefore, the national survey suggested that while EPs see neuropsychology as relevant to practice, their actual knowledge of the field is limited. Thus, while EPs may be in a strong position as a profession to challenge neuromyths in education, as noted in Chap. 2, their lack of familiarity with the field is likely to constitute a significant barrier to this process. The findings have also highlighted an important additional consideration—the comparatively low level of knowledge of neuropsychological theory and concepts amongst EPs can potentially be traced back to another key finding—the very limited teaching on neuropsychology during the initial EP training courses, as discussed in the next section.

Neuropsychology Teaching During the Initial EP Training: Views and Experiences

The national survey highlighted another important factor potentially contributing to the unexplored relationship between the two disciplines—the majority of participants (73%) indicated that they had not had any neuropsychology-focused teaching during their initial training as an EP. In contrast, 92% of respondents stated that they would have liked to have had input on neuropsychology. The reasons listed by participants were not restricted simply to a desire to learn more about an unfamiliar area; rather, most EPs were able to identify a range of situations in their day-to-day practice when they would be able to apply neuropsychological knowledge (e.g. training provision, challenging "neuromyths", complex casework). Some EPs, for example, highlighted the importance of having an understanding of brain function and brain-behaviour relationships:

> As a psychologist, understanding the role of the brain and how this impacts is essential, I feel that there isn't enough focus on this as we are scared to be associated with anything too medical.

Other EPs highlighted gaps in their knowledge that they believed could be addressed if neuropsychology teaching had been included in the initial training courses, particularly as they had encountered neuropsychological conditions such as epilepsy and acquired brain injury in their practice, but did not feel sufficiently confident in their knowledge: Another sub-theme that was identified referred to the relevance and application of neuropsychology for comprehensive formulations, alongside the use of systemic and environmental theories and considerations:

> I would like to have known more about the developing brain and its relationship with emotional responses and behaviour. Much of what we concentrate on are the things people have some control over (the system the child is living within, the relationships, the social dynamics etc) and this is important but it would be useful to have known more about some important within child factors too.

While 27% of EPs reported that they had neuropsychology-focused teaching during their initial training as EPs, their experiences varied widely depending on the focus of the teaching. The teaching sessions covered a broad range of topics, ranging from short single sessions covering a specific condition or an individual EP's experience of working in a neuropsychological setting, to more generic overview of brain development and specific assessment tools. The responses suggested that the majority of teaching was restricted to a single session that was largely focused on the facilitator's experience or interests, which may potentially result in very different experiences across different training providers.

Do EPs See Paediatric Neuropsychology as a Specialism Open to Them?

> If I had learnt more about neuropsychology as a TEP, pediatric neuropsychology might feel a bit more open to me as a possible career.

The majority of EPs (68%) indicated that they were not at all familiar or had very limited knowledge of paediatric neuropsychology as a separate training route and 75% had not considered training as a paediatric neuropsychologist. More than half (53%) of those who had considered training were maingrade EPs, and only 12% were trainees. In contrast, out of those who had not considered training, 40% were maingrade EPs and a further

38% were trainees and 16% were senior or Principal EPs. Therefore, it appears that training as a paediatric neuropsychologist is not as popular during the very early stages of an EP's career (i.e. during training) and towards the end of their career. Eighty per cent of respondents who indicated that they had not considered training as a neuropsychologist listed not knowing enough about the area or not knowing that training as a paediatric neuropsychologist was an option available to EPs as their reason.

Participants who had considered completing further specialist training in neuropsychology listed a number of reasons for wishing to further their knowledge in this area. Specifically, some wrote about a desire to add an extra dimension to their assessments and conceptualisation of the needs of the children they work with:

> It is impossible, and probably futile, to disentangle the brain from all of the other systems that affect child development; therefore, it makes sense to study it. Also, I find it endlessly fascinating and I am seeing more and more children whom I would like to have a better understanding of the neuropsychology and do a more in depth assessment.

Other respondents listed their interests in the evolving field of the neuro-disciplines and the scientific elements of neuropsychology as a factor that had provoked their interest in the area, alongside a longstanding personal interest in neuropsychology and neuroscience that remained active after they completed their training as an EP:

> I have an academic background and particular interest in Neuropsychology and I believe that it is extremely relevant to Educational Psychology practice, therefore I wish to understand it better. I would also like to be able to increase the neuropsychological understanding of professionals (such as education staff) that we work with.

In contrast, considering that only a quarter of all respondents had considered training in neuropsychology, it is important to explore the reasons why the remaining 75% had not considered that option. Lack of sufficient knowledge of the field emerged as the most significant factor, with 50% of the respondents stating that they were unaware of this option and a further 20% stating that they did not know enough about the area. The EPs also highlighted a number of additional reasons why they had not considered paediatric neuropsychology training. Those included current career stage, and particularly being close to retirement, which was listed by a number of EPs as a key factor making further training a less appealing option. Similarly, the time demands and cost associated with further training were highlighted as another barrier by some respondents, who noted that their employers would be unlikely to support them financially or in practical terms if they were to embark on further training. Some EPs also flagged up the lack of sufficient opportunities to apply neuropsychological knowledge in their current setting as another factor that made them less likely to consider training in neuropsychology:

> From discussions with EPs who have trained, I feel that the information and knowledge gained is very useful but that unless we can be seconded or work in a medical setting there is very limited relevance to our daily work at the current time.

Overall, the national survey has painted a complex picture of the perception of neuropsychology by EPs. Indeed, the survey highlighted that while neuropsychology is perceived as relevant to everyday practice by the majority of EPs, this is in sharp contrast to their self-reported knowledge of the field. More specifically, while over 70% EPs stated that they refer to neuropsychological concepts in their everyday practice, less than 20% of them felt confident in their knowledge about the differences between neuroscience and neuropsychology and less than 25% stated they had a good or very good knowledge of neuropsychology theory. This, combined with the fact that the majority of participants had not had any neuropsychology-focused teaching during their initial training as EPs and were not aware that EPs could specialise in neuropsychology, raises important questions about the visibility of neuropsychology, as well as about the discrepancy between the EPs' openness to incorporating neuropsychology in their practice, and the lack of information and teaching in this area.

The survey has also revealed that the content, depth and quality of neuropsychology-related teaching that has already been introduced on some initial training courses vary significantly. Most EPs noted that the teaching consisted of less than five hours of direct instruction and covered material ranging from an overview of neuropsychological principles, to discussions of assessment tools or discussions about the role of EPs in neuropsychology. This suggests that there is little consistency between different courses in terms of the content of the teaching, and therefore careful consideration needs to be given to the planning of these modules, as well as to the choice of facilitator in charge of developing and delivering the sessions.

To What Extent Do EPs Perceive Paediatric Neuropsychology Theory to Be Relevant to Educational Psychology Practice?

The national survey indicated that 65% of EPs thought that neuropsychology was relevant or extremely relevant to everyday EP practice and 73% indicated that they refer to neuropsychological concepts in their day-to-day practice. Similarly, 80% of respondents stated that they had worked on neuropsychological cases, with the figure rising to 90% amongst qualified EPs, yet only 22% of respondents stated that they felt confident about their theoretical knowledge when working on those cases. The sub-sample of participants who reported feeling "not at all confident" or "not confident" about their knowledge were evenly distributed in terms of their level of experience. This suggests that the participants' lack of confidence does not appear to be related to their experience levels (i.e. lower confidence levels amongst trainees or newly qualified EPs), but rather may be indicative of a broader lack of sufficient knowledge and understanding of this area, as already highlighted in the previous section.

The survey also provided data on the type of neuropsychological conditions EPs encounter in their practice, which is a topic that has not been investigated in the literature before. Epilepsy and acquired brain injury emerged as the most commonly encountered conditions of neurological origin in EPs' everyday practice, followed by brain tumours, Foetal Alcohol Spectrum Disorders, as well as stroke, cerebral palsy and encephalitis (Fig. 4.1). These data may be particularly beneficial to initial training providers, as well as educational psychology services considering the introduction of neuropsychological training with direct relevance to EPs' day-to-day practice, as they can provide suggestions for key areas of focus.

These findings provide additional nuance to the data outlined in the previous section—specifically, while neuropsychology is perceived as relevant to everyday EP practice and the majority of respondents stated they used neuropsychological concepts in their work, the respondents consistently indicated that they are not confident about their level of knowledge of neuropsychological theory. This finding emerged in relation to both generic applications of neuropsychology to non-neuropsychological cases, and neuropsychological cases EPs encounter in their practice. The significant gap between the EPs' use of neuropsychology and their reported knowledge raises questions about EPs' ability to apply knowledge of areas that they are not confident in. The next section aims to illuminate this further, by exploring the ways in which EPs believe they apply neuropsychological principles to their practice.

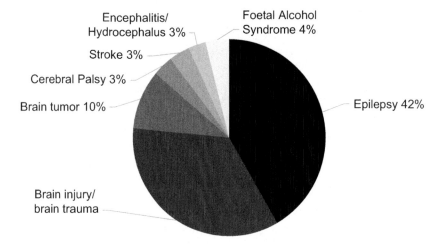

Fig. 4.1 Neuropsychological conditions EPs encounter in their everyday practice

How Does Neuropsychology Inform EPs' Day-to-Day Practice?

All EPs who indicated that they used neuropsychological concepts in their practice were given the opportunity to elaborate further with specific examples. One key area where neuropsychological knowledge was perceived as relevant by the respondents was early life cognitive and brain development, particularly in the context of consultation with schools and parents, with neuroplasticity being mentioned in a number of responses:

> I have made reference to concepts such as neuroplasticity and neuronal pruning over the course of development. The neurological changes resulting from literacy acquisition have been helpful in refuting predeterministic views of dyslexia.

> I will talk about creating new pathways in the brain, neuroplasticity and the fight or flight response.

However, as highlighted in Chap. 2, it is important to emphasise that there are critical issues that need to be explored when considering the use of neuro-concepts, especially in the absence of any prior training in neuroscience or neuropsychology. For example, while neuroplasticity is a legitimate scientific concept referring to the brain's ability to change, re-organise and form new neural connections in response to internal and external stimuli over the life course (Cramer et al., 2011), the term can be misinterpreted and used to justify far less scientific ideas. As noted by neurobiologist Moheb Constandi, neuroplasticity has become "a buzzword in many different realms" from the self-help industry, to the business world and education, where overexaggerated or inaccurate claims are made about the brain's ability to change or heal (Costandi, 2016). Thus, it is not clear whether EPs referring to similar terms in practice are always familiar with those broader debates and complexities, which highlights the need for teaching and training on those important topics.

Some respondents indicated that they use neuropsychological concepts in their daily practice to help children, parents and school staff make sense of the presenting difficulties in a non-pathologising way. This challenges some of the views about neuropsychology as outlined in previous chapters, where neuropsychology was seen as potentially promoting within-child and pathologising views of the child's difficulties:

> I use my understanding of neurodevelopment in children, especially teenagers, to normalise their behaviour, especially around sleep patterns.

A significant proportion of respondents indicated that they refer to neuropsychological concepts in the context of attachment-related difficulties, while others indicated that neuropsychology is a helpful reference point during the formulation process for complex cases, including cases where the child has a medical condition of neurological origin. Training provision was highlighted as another area where the respondents referred to and incorporated neuropsychological concepts. Specifically, the respondents spoke about using their knowledge of neuropsychological theory when delivering training on attachment and trauma, cognitive and executive function development. Finally, some EPs reported that they use neuropsychology to challenge or clarify misconceptions held by staff about neuropsychological concepts:

> Often I find that teachers are the ones that mention neuropsychological concepts—often with very little understanding and misinterpretation. Much of my role then becomes about clarifying the concepts and often pointing out their limited scope for information intervention.

This suggests that there is willingness amongst some EPs to engage in more critical discussions with schools about some of the challenges and limitations of neuropsychology's applications to education. However, considering the issues identified around EPs' own very limited knowledge of neuropsychological theory and concepts, some EPs may not feel or, indeed, may not be, appropriately equipped to have discussions of this nature or to challenge wrongly held assumptions by educators. Similarly, it is important to note that EPs should also be aware of the limitations to their own knowledge and competence, particularly when referring to neuroscientific or neuropsychological concepts if they have not had formal teaching or training in the area. This further highlights the need for any neuropsychology teaching or training courses for EPs to include information about common misconceptions and neuromyths, and how those can be challenged.

SUMMARY

The national survey responses identified a number of key findings, with significant implications for the understanding of the relationship between educational psychology and neuropsychology in the UK. The results highlighted that while over 70% of respondents use neuropsychological concepts and a further 65% believe that neuropsychology is relevant to day-to-day EP practice, only 20% reported having a good or high level of knowledge of child neuropsychology theory. Even more significantly, over 90% of qualified EP respondents indicated that they had worked with cases involving neuropsychological conditions; however only 22% stated that they were confident about their knowledge in those cases.

This appears to highlight the need for some neuropsychology-focused input during the initial stages of EP training, with over 90% of EPs stating that they would have liked to have received teaching on this topic during training. Similarly, the survey findings appear to challenge the belief held by some that neuropsychology promotes medicalised, within-child formulations, by providing initial evidence and examples of how EPs use neuropsychological concepts to challenge predeterministic or deficit-focused views of the child's presentation. One possible reason for this discrepancy may lie in the fact that the debates surrounding the relevance of neuropsychology to education appear to often be led by academics or researchers in the field, rather than EPs. The focus of these discussions, as is the case in Bruer's (1997) paper, can therefore fall on the applications of neuroscience or neuropsychology to broader educational topics such as improving classroom learning, where the direct links may be less clear, compared to the links between neuropsychology and developmental conditions EPs typically encounter in their practice. The national survey results also provided further insight into the types of neuropsychological conditions EPs encounter in their everyday practice, as well as the main practice areas EPs currently use neuropsychological concepts.

While the national survey has attempted to provide a generic overview of the knowledge of and attitudes towards paediatric neuropsychology amongst EPs in the UK, in the next chapter we will focus on the role of EPs who have chosen to specialise in neuropsychology and currently work in neuropsychological settings. We will then consider the implications of both studies in Chap. 6, with reference to specific implications for practice and the ongoing relationship between the two disciplines.

REFERENCES

Bruer, J. T. (1997). Education and the brain: A bridge too far. *Educational Researcher, 26*(8), 4–16.

Costandi, M. (2016). *Neuroplasticity.* MIT Press.

Cramer, S. C., Sur, M., Dobkin, B. H., O'brien, C., Sanger, T. D., Trojanowski, J. Q., & Chen, W. G. (2011). Harnessing neuroplasticity for clinical applications. *Brain, 134*(6), 1591–1609.

CHAPTER 5

The Specialist Role of the EP in Neuropsychological Settings

Abstract Following the broader exploration of the perceptions and applications of neuropsychology to everyday EP practice, this chapter will consider the role of the EP in specialist neuropsychological settings from multiple perspectives. These will be presented with reference to the findings of a research study that involved interviews with four specialist EPs and six healthcare professionals working alongside them in two child neuropsychology settings in England: a paediatric neurorehabilitation service and a setting offering support to children and young people with acquired brain injuries. The chapter will consider key questions such as the training route to qualification as a paediatric neuropsychologist and the challenges and opportunities this presents; the factors that influence EPs' decision to specialise in neuropsychology, as well as the role and unique contribution of the EP to specialist neuropsychology settings from the perspective of both the psychologists and the healthcare professionals working alongside them.

Keywords Clinical neuropsychologist • Specialism • Neuropsychological settings • Brain injury

© The Author(s), under exclusive license to Springer Nature
Switzerland AG 2020
E. Misheva, *Child Neuropsychology in Practice*,
https://doi.org/10.1007/978-3-030-64930-2_5

THE ROUTES TO QUALIFYING
AS A CLINICAL NEUROPSYCHOLOGIST

In order to consider the research findings in their broader context, it is important firstly to outline the route to qualifying as a neuropsychologist in the UK. It is also necessary to distinguish between clinical child/paediatric neuropsychologists and academic neuropsychologists. While the latter are academics who carry out research in child neuropsychology but do not practise as neuropsychologists, clinical child neuropsychologists are qualified clinical or educational psychologists[1] who have undertaken further post-qualification training and supervised practice in paediatric neuropsychology.

Currently, in order for a clinical or educational psychologist to enter the British Psychological Society's (BPS) Specialist Register of Clinical Neuropsychologists and to be eligible for full membership of the Division of Neuropsychology, a candidate will need to demonstrate competence in three main "dimensions"—knowledge, research and supervised practice (British Psychological Society, 2017). The knowledge dimension refers to the candidate's ability to demonstrate their understanding of a range of theories, research and their application to practice (e.g. neuropsychological development in children, assessment approaches, professional practice issues). The research dimension assesses the candidate's ability to conduct clinical neuropsychology-relevant research. Candidates who have completed a doctoral-level qualification in clinical or educational psychology on a relevant topic can apply for an exemption from this requirement. Finally, the supervised practice component refers to the completion of two years full-time or full-time equivalent clinical practice supervised by a qualified Clinical Neuropsychologist who is on the BPS Specialist Register of Clinical Neuropsychologists. The candidate is assessed via an oral examination and their clinical case portfolio.

At present, there are two main routes to qualify as a clinical neuropsychologist and entering the Specialist Register of Clinical Neuropsychologists. The first one is the BPS-facilitated Qualification in Clinical Neuropsychology (QiCN), where all candidates are expected to study and organise their supervision and practice arrangements independently, and undergo assessments or examinations related to the different dimensions via the QiCN. Another option available to candidates is to pursue some of the dimensions via a specialist university course accredited by the BPS. Examples

---

[1] At the time of publication in January 2021, the BPS Division of Neuropsychology announced that the neuropsychology qualification route would open to counselling psychologists, in addition to clinical and educational psychologists.

of this include the Postgraduate Diploma/MSc in Clinical Paediatric Neuropsychology at University College London, where the successful completion of the Postgraduate Diploma fulfils the knowledge dimension requirements and the completion of the full MSc—the knowledge *and* research dimensions. Bristol University has introduced a Certificate in Clinical Neuropsychology Practice, which supports candidates with the development of the practical competencies required for entry to the Specialist Register of Clinical Neuropsychologists.

The titles "clinical psychologist" and "educational psychologist" are protected titles in the UK but "neuropsychologist" is not. While entry to the BPS' Specialist Register of Clinical Neuropsychologists is restricted to practitioners who have satisfied all the dimensions outlined above, the BPS is not a statutory regulatory body in the same way the Health and Care Professions Council (HCPC) is. Similarly, while it would be an offence for an individual who is not registered with the HCPC to use practitioner psychologist's one of the protected titles, this would not currently be the case for the title "neuropsychologist".

ARE EPs UNDERREPRESENTED AMONGST CLINICAL NEUROPSYCHOLOGISTS?

As outlined in the section above, the training routes to becoming a clinical neuropsychologist and entering the BPS Specialist Register of Clinical Neuropsychologists are only open to qualified Clinical and Educational Psychologists (CPs/EPs). However, there are currently no publicly available data specifying the distribution of EPs and CPs within that broader group of psychologists.

In order to ascertain the representation of EPs amongst registered Clinical Neuropsychologists, the author contacted the British Psychological Society (BPS), requesting the number of clinical and educational psychologists on the Specialist Register of Clinical Neuropsychologists. The Society held no information about the distribution of EPs and CPs on the register and were only able to provide the total number of psychologists on it (418 practitioners at the time of writing). The author manually cross-referenced the individual psychologists on the BPS list with the HCPC registration records, in order to determine whether they were registered as a CP or an EP. This analysis indicated that EPs constitute just 2% of all registered neuropsychologists (409 of the 418 psychologists on the

Specialist Register were CPs, 2 psychologists had dual registration as CPs and EPs, but practiced as CPs, with the remaining 7 being EPs).

According to data provided by the HCPC, there are currently 4579 registered EPs and 13,381 registered CPs in the UK. Thus, as there are nearly three times as many CPs as there are EPs, it is expected that, proportionally, there will be a larger number of CPs on the Specialist Register of Clinical Neuropsychologists, where approximately 25% would be EPs and 75% would be CPs. However, as EPs currently constitute just 2% of the total clinical neuropsychologist population, they are severely underrepresented. A further analysis was carried out with the Clinical Neuropsychologists who specialise in working with children and adolescents, rather than adults, as EPs would not typically work exclusively with adult populations. Even within this subgroup, EPs were substantially underrepresented compared to CPs, as seen in Fig. 5.1.

WHAT FACTORS INFLUENCE EPS' DECISION TO SPECIALISE IN NEUROPSYCHOLOGY?

The national survey findings discussed in Chap. 4 indicated that neuropsychology is an area in which Educational Psychologists do not have a detailed level of knowledge, with the majority of participants stating that they were not aware of the training routes into neuropsychology open to EPs. The in-depth interviews with EPs working in neuropsychological

Fig. 5.1 Breakdown of child and adolescent neuropsychologists by professional background

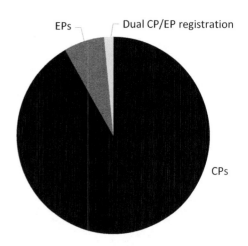

EPs

Dual CP/EP registration

CPs

settings provided an insight into the reasons and motivating factors leading to their decision to specialise in neuropsychology. While there was a degree of variability in the participants' responses depending on their distinct career trajectories and motivating factors, a number of common themes were identified. Specifically, the participants' responses fell within two broad categories—systemic factors leading to the increased presence of EPs in child neuropsychological settings, and individual factors, referring to person-specific circumstances that had led to a career as an EP working in neuropsychology.

Systemic Factors

Shifting Paradigms in Neuropsychology: Increased Recognition and Appreciation of EPs' Contribution to Child Neuropsychology

One systemic factor identified by the specialist EPs was the increased recognition of the role and contribution of EPs to child neuropsychology settings, particularly in light of the fact that the young person's cognitive development and education are a key focus of the rehabilitation process. Some participants reflected on the fact that, until recently, Educational Psychologists were not represented in neuropsychological settings, however there was now a growing appreciation of their contribution, thus recognising the need for EP involvement in this practice area:

> I think there's been a growing shift within neuropsychology generally. For a long time, I think educational psychologists essentially were kind of a new breed coming into neuropsychology and there was kind of this, "Oh, what is this—clinical neuropsychology, but yet, there's these educational psychologists!". And I think there's been a growing kind of appreciation of what educational psychologists can bring. (Educational Psychologist)

Similarly, the specialist EPs also reflected on how the role of the EP and their unique contribution is seen by health professionals in their settings:

> When I talk with clinical colleagues, they will often say it's our knowledge of the school system, our ability to work with schools and teachers and families to be able to kind of think about a holistic intervention plan that's reasonable, feasible, realistic, and with the young person's voice at the centre of it. Huge amount of the work that we will be doing will be thinking about schools as a future rehab setting, but thinking about the person's voice in

that, the things that are really important to them. How can we get that voice heard? And I think that's something that we've possibly added to the service. (Educational Psychologist)

The growing recognition of the importance of Educational Psychology input in child neuropsychology cases was also highlighted by the professionals working alongside the EPs, who reflected on the unique contribution Educational Psychologists have, compared to other professionals in the multidisciplinary team (MDT). Specifically, they reflected on the importance of having the opportunity to work alongside a professional who has an understanding of the education system, as well as:

[T]he knowledge of how schools work, and what is possible in a school setting. What are the policies and the guidelines that they have to adhere to, and how, and the kind of language to use to try and get the right support for the kids has been invaluable. Because even as an OT, yes, I have worked a lot in community services and with schools as well. But this is just a step up, because they know the systems so well, and also what it means for kids to learn and how you measure the learning and what the schools should be putting in place. (Occupational Therapist)

Individual Factors

In addition to changes in the systemic landscape in neuropsychology, a number of individual factors were highlighted by the EPs as having a key role in their decision to specialise in neuropsychology. While one participant reported having a pre-existing interest in brain-behaviour relationships, prior interest in neuropsychology per se did not emerge as a factor influencing the EPs' decision to work in a neuropsychological setting. Instead, the key individual factors that influenced the EPs' decision to specialise in neuropsychology fell in two broad categories: a strong interest in developing a specialism and a desire to explore new, more creative ways of working in a setting other than a local authority.

Desire to Have a Specialism and Job Availability at the Time of Application

A desire to have a specialism was highlighted as a key individual factor leading to the EPs' decision to apply for a job in a neuropsychological setting. The participants reflected on the fact that, having worked in a "generic", local authority-based Educational Psychologist role for a number of years, they were looking for opportunities to develop their skills further in a more specialist role. None of the specialist EPs reported looking for a role in neuropsychology specifically; rather, they were willing to explore a number of different avenues and the availability of an EP role in a neuropsychological setting at the time was a key factor that led them to explore this possibility further:

> *I was working for a local authority education service at that moment as an Educational Psychologist. I'd been there for quite a number of years and was just sort of feeling a little tired of the generic role. I wanted to think of things, how could I specialise.* (Educational Psychologist)

> *I had an alert for years ago on the NHS, and it just came through. And I thought, wow, I'd never heard of this team, and had a look at it a little bit more and thought that it would be a really good challenge. I'd always wanted to carve-out a type of area, like a specialism.* (Educational Psychologist)

Most EPs noted that they found out about the vacancy by chance or by having a pre-existing connection to the service, such as an ex-colleague or pre-qualification work experience in the same setting. The fact that the roles were not advertised on the website of the Association of Educational Psychologists where EPs would typically look for vacancies was raised by some as having implications for the visibility of these roles to EPs by restricting the pool of potential applicants.

Interest in Working in a Setting Other Than a Local Authority and a Desire to Explore New Ways of Working
Another individual factor that influenced the EPs' decision to apply for a role in a neuropsychological setting was their interest in developing new skills and ways of working outside of what was perceived as the more "traditional" local authority-based role of the EP:

> *I think there was something about working in a setting other than a local authority. I'd kind of got to the point where I had fantastic relationships with my schools, worked really well with them, but I wanted to kind of explore doing something different. And so when the post came up here, that was an opportunity to develop my skills.* (Educational Psychologist)

Similarly, some participants reflected on the fact that working in a neuropsychological setting provided them with more flexibility and time to explore new ways of working that they had limited opportunities to do in a local authority EP setting:

> *I think, historically, maybe not so much anymore, educational psychologists tend to be more local authority-based and that obviously comes with its own set of issues with the kind of bureaucracy and things like that. So here, for example, there's loads of intervention work, there's loads of assessment work, loads of parent support, so it's quite nice in that way. And also, we've got a massive benefit of just … time. Where the young people come for two to four months, and you might see them on a weekly basis, or twice weekly basis, over that time, you can just really develop that relationship and feel like you can see progress, whereas I found in local authority, where it's more consultation-based or you might do a one-off school visit, I found it sometimes quite hard that you never got as much of that follow-up.* (Educational Psychologist)

Overall, three main factors contributing to Educational Psychologists' decision to pursue specialist roles in neuropsychology were identified. On a systemic level, the participants identified the increased recognition of EPs' skills and expertise amongst other professionals as one factor leading to the availability of more employment opportunities for EPs in neuropsychological settings. On an individual level, the desire to develop a specialism and to explore working in a setting other than a local authority emerged as the two leading factors that influenced the participants' decision to apply for roles in neuropsychological settings.

The Role of the EP in Neuropsychological Settings

While the EPs who took part in the research had varying levels of experience and positions within their respective settings, ranging from a recently qualified EP to a head of service, a number of commonly occurring themes were identified. Specifically, all EPs worked as members of the wider multi- or interdisciplinary team and spoke about their role in bringing psychological understanding to the team, as well as challenging misconceptions and bridging the gap between education and health settings. The key areas of involvement for EPs in neuropsychological settings emerged as the assessment of need, reintegration, transition, psychoeducation, training, parent support, research and joint formulation.

Multidisciplinary Collaboration as a Key Component of Neuropsychological Practice: The EP's Role in Facilitating the Development of a Shared Understanding of the Child's Needs

All Educational Psychologists interviewed were based in multidisciplinary or interdisciplinary teams consisting of other educational and clinical psychologists, occupational therapists, speech and language therapists, physiotherapists, social workers and a medical doctor. The focus of their work was on supporting children with specific neurological conditions such as Acquired Brain Injury (ABI). While one of the settings worked exclusively with outpatients, the other offered residential rehabilitation stays for the children and young people it supported. All EPs interviewed described their role as being firmly positioned in the wider multi- or interdisciplinary team and focused around providing psychological advice to the team and the service users, as well as clarifying and supporting other professionals to make sense of the child's educational needs in the wider legislative and educational context:

> My role here is many things. So I guess one of the things, starting with the multidisciplinary team, is being part of the team. Having a shared perspective. So we start right at the beginning, helping the team formulate what's going on and having hypotheses about what's happening and getting shared understanding, but also keeping the multidisciplinary team in mind. So we often do (...) consultation for the team and joint working when it's appropriate as well. (Educational Psychologist)

Sharing Psychological Knowledge with the Multidisciplinary Team and Challenging Misconceptions

Using core EP skills (consultation, formulation and systemic working) to facilitate a psychological conceptualisation of the child's needs within the team, as well as challenging misconceptions, emerged as another key aspect of the EP role in neuropsychology. Specifically, the participants reflected on the fact that, considering the broad range of professional backgrounds in their teams, their knowledge of both psychology and education placed them in a strong position to both offer advice and deliver training in those areas:

> I think what I have brought really is an understanding about the systems that we work in, in terms of being EPs. I have done a lot of training with the team

in terms of the code of practice, the language that we use, how best to work with professionals, consultations, skills around working with schools. I think in terms of what makes me different is those things around the whole school aspect and understanding those processes, and the academic type side of things, and thinking about child development and typical development, and what that would look like. (…) we wanted to think about ways that we could work together more effectively with education, because we're health. (…) I have done a lot of training around literacy and reading and maths and school-based interventions— this is another thing that I've been able to share that knowledge with the team. (Educational Psychologist)

Some participants identified another aspect to their role—using their knowledge of cognitive development and assessment as EPs to challenge misconceptions about concepts such as IQ or the use of full-scale IQ scores:

There's still that sort of understanding that IQ says this and they would meet the criteria for a learning disability. And, well, actually, you know, this young person's functionally, is actually much better than that. So challenging in terms of, in the EP world, we wouldn't use full scale IQ. We would talk about description of needs and think about how they function and the environment. So that, I suppose, that's quite a bit different. (Educational Psychologist)

Educational Psychologist or Neuropsychologist? EP Identity in Multidisciplinary Teams

Another important theme highlighted in the research focused around the EP identity in neuropsychological settings. Specifically, the participants reflected on how their identity as an EP had in fact strengthened since joining their services, as they were either the only EP or one of the few EPs working in their setting alongside professionals from various other backgrounds:

I think when you work in neuropsych-type settings, you're often much more multidisciplinary team-based. And I actually think some people think, "Oh, you're going to lose your identity". But actually, I think it helps because you establish what you do against what someone else does and where the overlap is and where the differences are. And then I actually think that helps in terms of understanding your unique contribution. (Educational Psychologist)

Some EPs also reflected on the fact that they see neuropsychology as a specialism that adds to their role as an EP, rather than as a separate career path:

People would tend to say, "I'm an educational psychologist, and then I'm a neuropsychologist" or "I'm a clinical psychologist, and then I'm a neuropsychologist". And that is what I think—this is a kind of added part that you would then fit within all of your previous training, and it adds to it. But it couldn't be without the rest, if you see what I mean. And I think people maybe see it a bit on its own. (Educational Psychologist)

The EPs who worked alongside clinical psychologists identified a number of ways in which their practice was similar but also differed, so that they all had a distinct identity and focus of their work:

In my previous role, I'd worked knowing that there are clinical psychologists out there but didn't really know what their remit was. And of course working very closely, you start to see how, how we sort of almost morph into each other. But there are differences, similarities and differences. (…) The Ed Psychs, we do have a lot of experience and understanding of the educational world, of special educational needs in particular, of young people who are only here for a very transitory period in their rehab. They're coming from school, they're going back into school, they're coming from nursery, they're going to school. (Educational Psychologist)

The same participant elaborated further on how the EPs' knowledge of education and working closely with school settings, in combination with their knowledge of child development distinguishes them from CPs:

We have an understanding of teaching, learning, we have an understanding of development of cognition, etc. We're quite comfortable in school settings. So we can sort of do support, do transition visits quite easily. I think that's where the clinical psychologists say, "Yeah, you get over that bit, because that's not our comfort zone. (Educational Psychologist)

The clinical psychologist interviewed reflected on the fact that, while the roles of the educational and clinical psychologists in neuropsychology are similar, the clinical psychologists' work is more focused on supporting the young people and parents with mental health-related issues:

I feel like our roles are … the only time where I feel like I can see there is a slight difference when it comes to whether someone we're working with or parent really does fit with a mental health presentation. (Clinical Psychologist)

However, despite this distinction, some EPs noted that this does not mean that mental health-focused work would be "off-limits" for EPs, who remain involved in the provision of mental health and wellbeing-related support:

And so if they've got clinical kind of mental health need, it would tend to be the clinical psychologist. But if it's more about making sense of how things are for them kind of after their brain injury, then we get very involved in that as well. (Educational Psychologist)

What Is the Unique Contribution of EPs to Neuropsychology Practice? Perspectives from EPs and Multidisciplinary Professionals

EP Perspectives

The EPs interviewed reported a high level of skills transfer from their local authority-based EP role to their specialist role in neuropsychology and highlighted the relevance and importance of EP input to child neuropsychology. They reflected on the EP's key role in bringing their knowledge of the education system to teams that largely consisted of health professionals with limited links to education. This was perceived as particularly important, as returning to education and supporting the child's educational reintegration was highlighted as one of the key focus areas of the rehabilitation process. Similarly, as the children and young people often required input from a number of professionals and agencies, the EPs saw their skills and expertise in systemic thinking and working with other professionals as key to their role in neuropsychology.

Knowledge of Systems Theory and Experience of Working with Other Professionals and Settings

The EPs reported that their ability to bring systemic thinking to the multi-agency team, alongside their understanding of the child's broader educational needs, represented their specialist contribution to child neuropsychology practice, compared to other members of the multidisciplinary team:

I do think we're really trained to think quite systematically about how to approach kind of pieces of assessment tools and inform intervention. I think another massive thing with the paediatric neuropsychology population is, having some form of neuropsychological issue going on, whether it's an acquired brain injury or epilepsy, has a massive impact in terms of schooling, in terms of missed schooling, in terms of their cognitive function, in terms of how much of a sense of belonging they've got, if they feel quite different, you know, so many factors. (Educational Psychologist)

The same participant went on to reflect on the benefits of having a detailed understanding and experience of working with educational settings as an EP working in neurorehabilitation:

I think being education-based and having those good links with school and being able to think about how we support transition back to school or how we support a sense of belonging or a sense of identity within school or supporting the school's understanding, I think having that connection with school is really quite key in terms of supporting these young people at their base, where things can be coordinated. So I think the fact that we have good links to school and we're used to working with schools in a collaborative way, is another massive bonus to what we can bring. (Educational Psychologist)

Similarly, some participants saw their ability to make psychology accessible to other professionals and ability to formulate as the main contribution of EPs to neuropsychological practice:

I think educational psychologists are perfect for working in paediatric neuropsychology, because I think part of it is, big part of it is that kind of bio-psychosocial formulation—I think we're really well trained in formulation. (Educational Psychologist)

I think it's our ability to make psychology accessible to others, that also has led the kind of increase of educational psychology here, in a way that has felt non-threatening. It's felt supportive and it has enabled people to think, do you know what, psychology isn't scary. And psychology can be useful, it can be helpful. (Educational Psychologist)

Knowledge of the Education System, Child Development and Cognitive Development

The EPs also reflected on how their knowledge of the educational system and child development was a key contribution they could make in the context of child neuropsychology practice:

We do have a lot of experience and understanding of the educational world, of special educational needs in particular, of young people who are only here for a very transitory period in their rehab. They're coming from school, they're going back into school, they're coming from nursery, they're going to school. So we have that broader view of their previous experience, where they're going to. We have an understanding of teaching, learning, we have an understanding of development of cognition, etc. We're quite comfortable in school settings. So we can sort of do support, do transition visits quite easily.

As Ed Psychs, I think we're really, really well-placed to work with these young people and to be supporting young people who've had neurological conditions— we see them all the time in schools. (Educational Psychologist)

Additionally, the EPs reflected on how their knowledge of the educational system and systemic working skills were valued by the rest of the team:

They've been really welcoming and really interested in some of the things that I have to say, and my experiences that I have in terms of education, systems and processes, but also thinking about other ways of assessment. (Educational Psychologist)

"She Knows a Language I Don't Know": Multidisciplinary Professionals' Perspectives on EPs' Role and Contribution to Child Neuropsychology Practice

The allied healthcare professionals working alongside EPs in their respective settings provided further insight into the role and unique contribution of EPs to child neuropsychology. Overall, they all spoke at length about the benefits and importance of having an EP in the multidisciplinary team and the range of contributions EPs make to the service.

EPs' Role in Supporting the Multidisciplinary Team with Psychological Thinking and Interventions

Some multi-agency professionals saw the EPs as having a key role in supporting the team to think psychologically and in more depth about the often very complex needs of the children and young people supported by the service:

The psychology team as a whole, so the educational psychologists and clinical psychologists, at the moment are very much leading our formulation meetings where we come together and talk about why, how the kids are presenting, some of the reasons for this and how, as a team, we're going to work with them to progress them to the goals that they want to achieve. (…) I think they are a really valuable member of the team, (…) they are able to get to the bottom of what the kids really need to be able to succeed in education. And more than that, they very much support us as a team to get the best out of the children. (Physiotherapist)

Contribution to Joint Working and Liaison between the Health Setting and the Child's School

Some MDT professionals highlighted the role of the EP in facilitating effective communication and transition from the neurorehabilitation settings to the child's school. Specifically, they spoke about their collaboration with the EP in those instances:

The work that I've done with educational psychologists has been a lot around returning to school or returning to the school setting. We've done school visits, seeing how schools set up providing that kind of brain injury education to the school, and giving them kind of helpful tips and strategies on how to work with the young person. I've done a couple of joint discharge planning meetings with EPs. Obviously it's quite helpful for there to be an educational psychologist in those, so someone that can feedback on how they've performed on different assessments and feedback where their skills lie or where their difficulties lie alongside our assessment. So it's very helpful and collaborative. (Occupational Therapist)

Knowledge of the Education System

The role of the EP in bridging the gap between health and education was highlighted as another important contribution they made to their respective settings. MDT members reflected on the fact that they had limited understanding of the education sector, yet reintegration back to school was a key focus of the rehabilitation process and as such, EPs had an important role in facilitating that process:

I find it extremely useful, because she knows a language I don't know, which is the language of education. I feel like she bridges the gap between schools and teachers and health professionals that maybe we can't do. (…) When we go and work together, we both bring something different to the table. So I'll say something, and then maybe she can translate it in a way that makes sense to the teachers. And I think that I can see maybe the training's changed over time cause obviously when I started working, Educational Psychologists were teachers as well and now they don't have to do that. So it feels more like I'm working with a psychologist now. Before, back in the day, it felt more like almost like a specialist teaching type of role. (Speech and Language Therapist)

Some MDT professionals spoke about the specific knowledge of a range of educational processes that EPs had that other professionals in the team did not have:

> *the knowledge of how schools work, and what is possible in a school setting. What are the policies and the guidelines that they have to adhere to, and how, and the kind of language to use to try and get the right support for the kids has been invaluable. Because even as an OT, yes, I have worked a lot in community services and with schools as well. But this is just a step up, because they know the systems so well, and also what it means for kids to learn and how you measure the learning and what the schools should be putting in place.* (Occupational Therapist)

Similarly, a clinical psychologist (CP) spoke about the differences in knowledge between EPs and CPs with reference to the education system, highlighting the unique contribution of EPs when compared to CPs:

> *(EPs have) a knowledge of support systems that are out there, how things work, the legislation side of things, or the systemic stuff. I think, as a clinical psychologist, okay, well, this is how we should adapt things, but in terms of their knowledge base of the education system, the legislation that goes with that, funding, EHCP plans. all of that type of stuff (…), you can see that that is the boundary compared to a clinical psychologist's knowledge. So I think particularly when it comes to recommendations and thinking about the person being discharged, you can see how knowledgeable educational psychologists are, in terms of how they communicate that across as well.* (Clinical Psychologist)

Holistic View of the Child in the Context of Their Neuropsychological Needs

Finally, the multi-agency team professionals highlighted the role of the EP in encouraging the team to see a holistic view of the child, where their neuropsychological needs are considered in the broader context of the child's environment, educational needs and general wellbeing:

> *being able to really see a holistic view of the child and what they are able to do and how to maximise what they're seeing, to kind of put in the support and the environment and the structures to meet their needs.* (Physiotherapist)

> *I would say the assessments that they do very much hone in on the young person's skills, where a speech therapist might look at how they do in certain reading assessments and their understanding of language in those assessments. Where,*

as OTs, we might look at their handwriting. And I feel like the Ed Psych assessments really hone in on other skills that are really important for school that we don't completely capture (...) So somebody who really works kind of supporting them through this new education journey and helping them find a setting has been really important and I think valued, they really pull all of that together and have that holistic idea of the young people and school needs. (Occupational Therapist)

Misconceptions About Neuropsychology Amongst Educational Psychologists Encountered by EPs in Neuropsychology

Another major theme identified from the participants' interviews concerned the perceived misconceptions about neuropsychology amongst EPs. The Educational Psychologists specialising in neuropsychology spoke about the misconceptions they had encountered from other EPs about both neuropsychology as a discipline, as well as about the role of EPs in neuropsychology (Fig. 5.2).

Perceptions of Neuropsychology as "Within-Child" and "Reductionist"

All EPs spoke about what they saw as one of the main misconceptions about neuropsychology in the profession—specifically, that neuropsychology promotes a reductionist, within-person model of the child's difficulties:

I think sometimes people worry that it's a bit reductionist, and everything comes down to, "the brain tells us to do this, so we do this". But actually, the course and all my learning so far has really set it in a bio-psycho-social model. That actually, that is part of the picture, but not all of the picture. But why would you not want to know more about that chunk to help you inform the whole thing? (Educational Psychologist)

Some participants reflected on how their own misconceptions about neuropsychology had been challenged since they started working in neuropsychological settings:

Now that I'm here, I think that some of my misconceptions about what would be going on actually have been really challenged because it's not all within child, actually, we do a lot of systemic interventions. Thinking about that, Bronfenbrenner—we do all of that. Sometimes we start from the outside in. (Educational Psychologist)

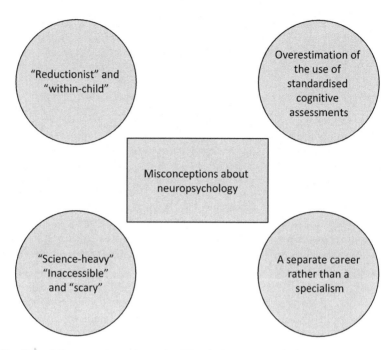

Fig. 5.2 Misconceptions about the EP role in neuropsychology

The EPs also spoke about the importance of adopting a broader systemic approach when working with children with brain injuries in contrast to the reductionist views about the practice of neuropsychology she had encountered and had held herself:

In terms of what I thought neuropsychology was, in terms of what we talked about in uni, I think that the reality of that is actually quite different. I think the perception was that it was all within-child, and it was the child's problem. And that you can go and find out what's wrong with this child. But actually I think in reality, people understand that it's way more complex than that. And especially for children with brain injuries. So yes, they might have had a brain injury, but actually, so many things that can happen environmentally that can support the child, they're way more important than delivering interventions about the child, thinking about the systems that are around that child and who is best to do that. (Educational Psychologist)

Overestimation of the Use and Reliance on Standardised Cognitive Assessments in Neuropsychology

Another key point raised in all interviews concerned the perception that neuropsychology practice is heavily reliant on the use of standardised cognitive assessments, with little scope for systemic thinking or more creative approaches to assessment and intervention:

> *Probably the biggest misconception is that neuropsychology is about doing some kind of standardised assessment with a list of recommendations. Whereas I would argue that neuropsychology is about having the understanding of the brain, thinking about what happens at different stages through development, how that informs your kind of formulation, and how you combine the links between what we know about the brain and the behaviours and all the other interactions that we see, to then support your psychological thinking. So I think that's possibly the biggest misconception, that people think it's about standardised testing and a lack of flexibility in that.* (Educational Psychologist)

Two other EPs reported similar experiences, where they found that EPs associated the role with an overreliance on cognitive assessments:

> *I think that people think it's all about cognitive testing, that neuropsychologists don't necessarily think of other factors other than just the brain-behaviour relationship. And so I think sometimes people think it's a bit reductionist and that it doesn't sit very well within a social-constructionist stance, where the issue is the issue and not the person.* (Educational Psychologist)

> *When I worked in a local authority, suddenly, when I got this job, people then kept coming to ask me questions about psychometric tests. So I was a bit like, why me?* (Educational Psychologist)

Perception of Neuropsychology as "Science-Heavy", "Inaccessible" and "Scary"

Some EPs spoke about neuropsychology's "reputation" as a highly technical, complex and science-heavy discipline, which leads some EPs to perceive it as "inaccessible" and "scary":

> *I do think there's just loads of misconceptions, and maybe people are a bit scared of it, because it feels quite sciency, but also, it's just a lot of unknowns. And there's a lot of myths about neuro-kind of stuff around how much of your brain you use, for example, and things like that. So I think that sometimes it feels a bit scary.* (Educational Psychologist)

*I think that does scare some people, you know, you just sort of think that it's dif-
ficult to understand perhaps.* (Educational Psychologist).

Perception of Neuropsychology as a Separate Discipline and Career, Rather Than as a Specialism

Another misconception identified by the participants referred to the view that neuropsychology is a separate career, which fails to acknowledge that child neuropsychologists need to be qualified Educational Psychologists first and will thus bring all their prior experiences and skills to the practice of neuropsychology:

*People would tend to say, "I'm an educational psychologist, and then I'm a
neuropsychologist" or "I'm a clinical psychologist, and then I'm a neuropsychologist". And that is what I think—this is a kind of added part that you
would then fit within all of your previous training, and it adds to it. But it
couldn't be without the rest, if you see what I mean. And I think people maybe
see it a bit on its own.* (Educational Psychologist)

Views on Training as a Paediatric Neuropsychologist

The participants interviewed as a part of the research all worked as EPs in neuropsychology, with two of them completing their additional training in order to qualify as paediatric neuropsychologists. All EPs reflected on the different training routes; while some participants wanted to eventually qualify as paediatric neuropsychologists, others were not interested in pursuing the qualification route and instead identified other professional development options that would enhance their role in neuropsychology further.

The University-Facilitated Route Perceived as More Affordable, Flexible and Accessible Compared to the BPS-Facilitated Qualification

Two of the four EP participants were in the process of completing the qualification in paediatric neuropsychology, which would enable them to enter the BPS register of qualified neuropsychologists. The EPs were both enrolled on a university-based course in paediatric neuropsychology, rather than pursuing the qualification (QICN) via the BPS. They identified the reduced cost and additional support associated with being linked to a university as the main factors that influenced their decision to undertake the university-supported route to the qualification:

It's cheaper. It also feels a bit more accessible, there's a lot more flexibility in it. And the conversations that I've had around QiCN, it doesn't feel like perhaps there's as much support. Whereas the (…) course has set up kind of those, more of those peer support networks. There is a bit of a structure and a framework to it; it's linked to a university. (…) I think the BPS is currently reviewing what will happen with QiCN. Because effectively QiCN is still meant to be the gold standard. But when the gold standard is a lot more expensive, and doesn't necessarily provide the same things, it's giving them something to think about. (Educational Psychologist)

Some of the participants noted that, regardless of the preferred qualification route, a significant financial investment is required in order to cover the course and supervision cost and employer support was highlighted as an important factor:

I've been very lucky. When I worked in local authority, they paid me to do the UCL course, I then halfway through the course cut down my hours with them, came here and they took on the funding for my second year there. And then the reason I'm doing the rest, of course, is because I was offered funding from here to do it. So I have been very lucky that I've been funded. They pay 80% and we're expected to pay 20%. So financially, I have been supported, which I know, again, is quite lucky, compared to people who've just had to self-fund. (Educational Psychologist)

Alternative Professional Development Options for EPs in Neuropsychology

Some EPs felt they would rather undertake training in areas such as family therapy or cognitive behavioural therapy, as they felt that this would be more beneficial to their day-to-day role. One of the EPs reflected specifically on why she felt that undertaking the neuropsychology qualification was not a priority for her, in the context of her role:

At the minute, it's not something that I feel able to do. And that's not to say that I won't do it. But actually, in terms of what I see my development in this role is, I would rather do additional training in family therapy, or CBT which is a possibility here. There's an opportunity for me to become ADOS-trained as well. And so that would be more interesting to me than doing a neuropsychology Master's, I think at this point. (Educational Psychologist)

Summary

The specialist role of EPs working in neuropsychological emerges as varied and multi-faceted, and entails a significant element of collaboration with multidisciplinary team members, brings knowledge of both psychology and education to predominantly healthcare-focused settings and bridges the gap between health and education. The EP's input was seen as highly relevant and important by the allied health professionals interviewed for the research, who spoke about the important added value EPs bring to the team with their systemic working skills, knowledge of both psychology and education, and the ability to consider a range of broader factors that may be impacting children's presentation.

Additionally, the specialist EPs' accounts have provided further insight into the common misconceptions EPs specialising in neuropsychology encounter about their roles, as well as the challenges and opportunities associated with clinical neuropsychology training. The next chapter will consider some of those key issues in the context of the future relationship between the two disciplines, with reference to the main research findings presented in Chaps. 4 and 5.

Further Reading

- Additional information about the Qualification in Clinical Neuropsychology (QiCN), including the Candidate Handbook that contains a detailed outline of the qualification process, can be found on the British Psychological Society's website

  https://www.bps.org.uk/psychologists/society-qualifications/qualification-clinical-neuropsychology

Reference

British Psychological Society. (2017). *Qualification in clinical neuropsychology: Candidate handbook*. Retrieved from https://www.bps.org.uk/sites/bps.org.uk/files/Qualifications/QICN%20Candidate %20Handbook%202018.pdf

The Future Relationship of EPs and Neuropsychology: Key Implications and Critical Issues

Abstract This final chapter will consider some of the key and most pertinent issues to the current relationship between educational psychology and child neuropsychology as identified by the research. First, it will consider what factors may have contributed to neuropsychology's reputation as an inaccessible and intimidating discipline, and how those barriers can be addressed in the future. Similarly, it will explore why EPs are currently underrepresented amongst clinical neuropsychologists, followed by a discussion of EPs' unique contribution to neuropsychological settings. Finally, it will consider common misconceptions about this specialist role and will conclude with a model framework for the various levels of engagement with neuropsychology EPs may have depending on their levels of experience, training and interest in the area.

Keywords Representation • Accessibility • Child neuropsychology • Educational psychologists • Specialism

© The Author(s), under exclusive license to Springer Nature Switzerland AG 2020
E. Misheva, *Child Neuropsychology in Practice*,
https://doi.org/10.1007/978-3-030-64930-2_6

79

DE-MYSTIFYING NEUROPSYCHOLOGY: WHY IS NEUROPSYCHOLOGY PERCEIVED AS INACCESSIBLE AND INTIMIDATING?

Neuropsychology intimidates me so I wanted to overcome that. However, since learning more about it, I wonder whether I have sufficient scientific knowledge to enter training. I have no science A Levels and studied psychology at masters level. There was some neuropsychology content and it was this that made me feel intimidated! I wish I could learn more about it but I don't think I have the skills and knowledge to engage at the required level. (National survey respondent)

.

The perception of neuropsychology as a highly complex and difficult to access discipline that requires significant background knowledge of biology emerged as a recurring theme from both the national survey responses, as well as the interviews with EPs working in specialist settings. This perception is also reflected in the academic literature, where the study of brain-behaviour relationships has been described by some as "remarkably compelling and at the same time incredibly overwhelming" (Hale & Fiorello, 2004). Hale and Fiorello (2004) also described disciplines concerned with brain-behaviour relationships as "difficult for professors to teach, students to learn, and practitioners to implement" and identified four key factors that may contribute to neuropsychology's perception as a highly complex and inaccessible discipline:

1. *Complex medical or biological terminology*—academic textbooks and courses in neuropsychology can contain a significant amount of subject-specific jargon which can become a barrier to psychologists' willingness or ability to meaningfully engage with the literature. This may also further consolidate neuropsychology's "reputation" as a medical or biological, rather than a psychological sub-discipline.
2. *Depth of coverage*—Hale and Fiorello (2004) argued that neuropsychology texts include a large amount of information related to brain anatomy, neurochemistry and the biology of brain function, which can be unnecessarily detailed and of little direct relevance to practise.
3. *Techniques used in neuropsychological research*—many neuropsychology research papers may include findings from neuroimaging techniques such as functional magnetic resonance imaging (fMRI) or

positron emission tomography (PET). As psychologists may have limited understanding of these techniques, this may affect their confidence and ability to both fully understand and critically evaluate any studies that have used neuroimaging, and consequently result in reluctance to refer to original empirical research in neuropsychology.

4. *Application of neuropsychological thinking and principles to practise*— Hale and Fiorello (2004) argued that many neuropsychology courses may have an overwhelming focus on the biological and physiological basis or behaviour, with limited direct applications to the practice of psychologists working with children. Thus, they emphasised the importance of ensuring that neuropsychology courses for psychologists working in education are taught by practitioners with expertise in child neuropsychology.

The perceived over-emphasis on biological concepts with limited direct application to practise is of relevance to another key point highlighted by the research—the distinction between neuroscience and neuropsychology. The national survey results suggest that there appears to be widespread confusion and lack of clarity regarding the differences between the two disciplines, with the terms often being used interchangeably. However, understanding this distinction is important when considering the relationship between neuropsychology and educational psychology, as the existing confusion may be contributing further to neuropsychology's reputation as an inaccessible discipline. It is therefore important to consider how the two disciplines differ in terms of their focus and scope. Neuroscience is concerned with the study of structure and function of the brain and nervous system (Purves et al., 2018), and is primarily an academic, rather than a practice discipline. As such, neuroscientific literature may be focused on examining the biological, anatomical and chemical processes behind a range of functional cognitive and behavioural processes. While a background and an interest in science is certainly going to be helpful for those EPs considering further training in neuropsychology, particularly with some aspects of the qualification's knowledge component (e.g. developmental cognitive neuroscience; development of sensory, motor and neural systems), neuropsychology is a sub-discipline of psychology, rather than biology, that examines brain-behaviour relationships. Thus, understanding the structure of the nervous system on the cellular and neurochemical level is one component, rather than the key focus of neuropsychology. Therefore, while the two disciplines are related, it is important that "neuroscience" and "neuropsychology" are not used as interchangeable terms, as this may further contribute to the existing confusion and perception of neuropsychology as a primarily biological or medical discipline amongst some EPs.

In order to address those barriers and points of confusion, there are a number of steps and considerations that Educational Psychology Services and universities may wish to take into account. Educational Psychology Services in the process of introducing professional development training in child neuropsychology, as well as universities offering courses or modules on neuropsychology, should consider carefully the course content. The data derived from the present research can inform these decisions in a number of ways. Firstly, the course content should be targeted rather than generic in nature, with a focus on understanding brain-behaviour relationships in the developing, as opposed to the adult brain. As outlined in the literature review in Chap. 1, this is a particularly important distinction for practitioners working with children, like EPs, as models about the function of the adult brain cannot be generalised and applied to the dynamic context of the developing brain (Reed & Warner-Rogers, 2009). This research has highlighted the most common neurological conditions EPs are likely to encounter in their practice, and the courses may therefore wish to introduce more in-depth teaching on these conditions (epilepsy, acquired brain injury, brain tumours, foetal alcohol spectrum disorders and cerebral palsy).

Additionally, course providers may wish to place the focus of the teaching on practice-related issues and minimise teaching on areas that are less relevant to direct practice, such as biological basis of brain function and neurochemistry. As highlighted in the literature, and specifically by Hale and Fiorello (2004), the inclusion of biological and physiological concepts and terminology is of limited direct relevance and usefulness to the practice of practitioners like EPs, yet it is one of the main contributing factors to the "reputation" of neuropsychology as an inaccessible discipline that ultimately deters practitioners from engaging with neuropsychology teaching modules.

EPs as Paediatric Neuropsychologists: Barriers and Opportunities

If I had learnt more about neuropsychology as a TEP pediatric neuropsychology might feel a bit more open to me as a possible career. (National survey respondent)

The national survey results indicated that nearly 70% of EPs were not at all aware or had very limited knowledge of the fact that EPs could train as child neuropsychologists and the training routes available. Similarly, less than a quarter had considered training as a paediatric neuropsychologist. The majority of those who had not considered training listed being unaware of this option as the main reason why they had not explored this possibility. Thus, it appears that neuropsychology training is not a visible professional development training option for EPs, considering that the majority of EPs had not had any neuropsychology-related training and most were unaware that this option existed. Training as a child neuropsychologist emerged as a more popular option amongst maingrade EPs, who constituted 53% of the participants who had considered training, and was less popular amongst those at the very early stages of their career and amongst senior and principal EPs. A number of external factors that had negatively affected some participants' ability to train were also highlighted, such as a lack of financial support by their employer or unwillingness to provide the appropriate study time, as well as being close to retirement age.

This indicates that, while the child neuropsychology training route is open to EPs, there are a number of barriers that restrict EPs' access to this specialism and may partially explain their proportionately lower representation amongst neuropsychologists, compared to Clinical Psychologists. Lack of awareness of the existence of this training option and qualification route emerged as a key factor restricting EPs' representation in the field. It is important to consider this in the context of the broader debates surrounding the perception of the neuro-disciplines as medicalised or promoting reductionist, within-person perspectives, as outlined in previous chapters. In this context, it is possible that some initial training courses may be reluctant to include neuropsychology teaching as this may be seen as promoting individualistic models of working that position the problem or difficulty within the child. However, another possible reason may be that the very limited number of EPs who have specialised in neuropsychology makes it challenging for training providers to find EPs with suitable experience and qualifications to teach. This, in turn, may result in a self-perpetuating cycle where lack of awareness of this specialism option leads to low representation of EPs in neuropsychology, as illustrated by Fig. 6.1.

Why Are EPs Underrepresented Amongst Qualified Neuropsychologists?

The interview findings have provided an insight into a range of additional factors that may contribute to the lower representation of EPs amongst registered clinical neuropsychologists. None of the EPs who took part in the research were qualified as clinical neuropsychologists and they are all employed as EPs. However, they had all considered further training as a clinical neuropsychologist and two of them were currently pursuing the practice dimension via an accredited university course, having completed the knowledge dimension via a university in the past. One EP noted that she was not interested in pursuing the qualification as she felt that further training in therapeutic work would be more beneficial to her specific role and setting. Another EP had considered this option as her employer was in a position to offer funding, but had ultimately decided against it due to being close to retirement age.

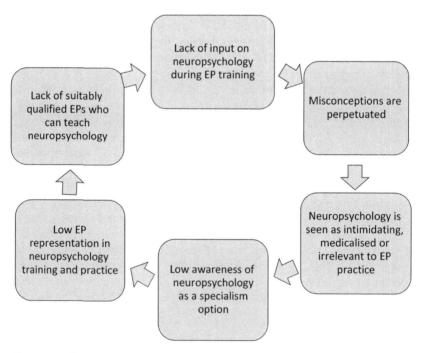

Fig. 6.1   The cycle of low EP representation in neuropsychology

The financial commitment associated with the qualification and whether employers would be willing to offer funding support was raised as a significant factor in the EPs' decision whether to pursue the qualification or not. Some EPs noted that the cost associated with undertaking the qualification is significant irrespective of the training route, with fees for a university-facilitated course meeting the knowledge and research dimension alone being in excess of £10,000. Similarly, the EPs noted that arranging clinical supervision by a qualified neuropsychologist can be another very significant expense, thus making self-funding prohibitive for many potential candidates. Another consideration raised by the EPs pursuing the qualification was the level of support and structure offered during the completion of the qualification, with the independent BPS route being seen as offering less support and structure, but at the same time being more expensive than the university-facilitated options.

This suggests that the current qualification process presents a number of barriers to prospective candidates. Firstly, the significant cost and lack of a clear funding model may deter EPs already working in neuropsychological settings from enrolling, unless they can secure funding from their employer. Another potential barrier highlighted by the research is the perceived lack of sufficient structure and support on the independent BPS qualification route, which made the university-facilitated options more appealing to the EPs. However, considering that standalone courses covering the three dimensions are offered by different universities, it is possible that this may lead to compartmentalisation of the qualification process, which may in turn appear overly complicated and thus deter potential candidates. Similarly, considering the widespread lack of awareness and confusion regarding the availability of neuropsychology as a specialism for EPs as identified in the national survey, the qualification route in its current form may add further confusion for EPs who are considering this specialism option.

CHALLENGING MISCONCEPTIONS ABOUT THE SPECIALIST ROLE AND PRACTICE OF EPs WORKING IN CHILD NEUROPSYCHOLOGICAL SETTINGS

As highlighted by the research findings presented in Chap. 5, not all EPs who work in neuropsychological settings are or, indeed, wish to qualify as Clinical Neuropsychologists, as it is possible to practise as a specialist EP in neuropsychological settings without any further qualifications. The role of the EP in neuropsychology emerged as multi-faceted and diverse, with the specific day-to-day responsibilities varying from one specialist setting to another. However, while there was a degree of variability in the nature of the EP's role depending on the context, the participants' accounts had a number of overlapping characteristics. Specifically, all EPs noted that they worked as part of a wider multi- or interdisciplinary team and would be actively involved in or leading the assessment and formulation process. The EP also had a key role in offering training, therapeutic work and parent and school liaison. This is in line with Reilly and Fenton (2013) and Ball and Howe (2013)'s findings—both studies highlighted the broad role and contribution of the EP in cases of epilepsy and acquired brain injury, and emphasised the role of EPs in supporting parents, school staff and multidisciplinary professionals, thus bridging the gap between health and education.

However, the research findings also suggested that the role of the EP in neuropsychology is poorly understood in the profession and the specialist EPs all spoke about a number of misconceptions they had encountered about their role. These ranged from beliefs held by other EPs that a specialist role in neuropsychology would be primarily focused on the administration of standardised cognitive assessments, to views that such roles would promote "reductionist" and "within-child" models of working.

This is in sharp contrast to the view of the EPs working in neuropsychology who noted that, while different in many respects, their specialist role involved many of the same skills they used in their local authority roles, but applied in a different context. All EPs who were interviewed emphasised that they still worked as an educational psychologist and identified as one, and noted that their identity as an EP had in fact strengthened in the specialist service. The EPs, including those who were currently undergoing further training as neuropsychologists, noted that this does not take away their identity as an EP. They saw neuropsychology training as a specialism, rather than as an alternative role or a career change, which is in contrast to how neuropsychology was perceived by some national survey respondents who saw it as a separate career route. In order to better understand and contextualise the high level of skill transfer between the local authority-based EP role and the role of the EP specialising in neuropsychology, it may be helpful to consider international perspectives on how the role of the EP and that of the neuropsychologist are similar and different.

THE ROLES OF THE EDUCATIONAL PSYCHOLOGIST AND PAEDIATRIC NEUROPSYCHOLOGIST IN THE UK: MORE SIMILAR THAN FIRST THOUGHT?

The role of the EP in the UK appears to be more closely associated with the role of the Paediatric Neuropsychologist in countries such as the United States and France, as opposed to the role of the school psychologist. More specifically, the National Association of School Psychologists in the United States describes school psychologists as "members of the school team" typically based in the school, who support the teachers' ability to teach and students' ability to learn, and are also responsible for managing behaviour, monitoring student progress, collecting and interpreting classroom data and reducing inappropriate referrals to external agencies (National Association of School Psychologists, 2019). As such, the school psychologist role in the countries in question encompasses responsibilities typically associated with the role of the Special Educational Need Coordinator (SENCO) and school counsellors in the UK.

In contrast, the American Academy of Clinical Neuropsychology defines the role of paediatric neuropsychologists as one that incorporates identifying the child's profile of strengths and weaknesses from a cognitive, as well as academic perspective, as opposed to the role of school psychologists, who are likely to focus on the child's academic attainment:

> *Pediatric neuropsychologists and school psychologists often use some of the same tests. However, school evaluations focus on deciding if a child has a problem with academic skills such as reading, spelling, or math. Pediatric neuropsychologists focus on understanding why a child is having problems in school or at home. This is done by examining academic skills but also examining all of the thinking skills needed to perform well in and outside of school—skills like memory, attention, and problem-solving.* (American Academy of Clinical Neuropsychology, 2019)

From this perspective, it can be argued that the role of the EP in the UK is broader and more specialist than its equivalents in other countries, and UK-trained EPs are already familiar with and use some of the skills, assessment tools and approaches relevant to paediatric neuropsychology practice, as highlighted by a number of participants in the interviews. This offers one possible explanation as to why Educational Psychologists in the UK who practise in neuropsychological settings reported high levels of skill transfer from their day-to-day role as a local authority EP to a more specialist neuropsychological setting. However, it is important to emphasise that this does *not* suggest that the roles of the EP and the paediatric clinical neuropsychologist in the UK are identical. Indeed, as discussed in Chap. 5, the EPs practising in neuropsychological settings all reflected on the fact that while they were familiar and able to use certain assessment tools and techniques (cognitive assessments, systemic working), they did still need to develop both their knowledge base and their ability to interpret their findings from a neuropsychological perspective:

> *There's nothing in there particularly that I couldn't do as an EP working in a local authority. (…)Probably the biggest difference is that, yes, an EP can do all those assessments, but do they know how to interpret them? Can they make that link between the brain biology and mechanisms and the behaviour that we're seeing? And I think that, you know, prior to coming here, I could do that on a basic level. I could say that (…) this child has difficulties around executive function and I might do some assessment around executive function to back that up (…) and I could maybe give some strategies for that. But I couldn't probably do anything beyond that.* (Educational Psychologist)

Thus, while the roles of the EP and the neuropsychologist in the UK are distinct, it appears that there is a significant overlap and a shared foundation between the two disciplines, which is not necessarily the case in other countries. The present research has also highlighted that neuropsychology is seen as a specialism, rather than a separate career path by EPs working in neuropsychological settings, and that these practitioners retain a strong identity as EPs.

The Unique Contribution of EPs to Child Neuropsychology Settings

The interviews carried out with EPs working in neuropsychology settings and healthcare professionals working alongside them provided a detailed account of the specialist contribution of EPs in a neuropsychological context, from multiple perspectives. The national survey and interview findings highlighted a discrepancy in attitudes and perceptions between how EPs see neuropsychology and the EP's role in this field, and how their role is perceived by healthcare professionals working in neuropsychological settings. The national survey findings suggested that some EPs are "scared to be associated with anything too medical" and have a very limited under-standing of the specialist roles EPs can undertake in neuropsychological settings. The findings indicated that, on the whole, EPs are not aware that this is a specialism that is open to them or where their expertise is required. In contrast, the healthcare professionals interviewed for the research highly valued the EP's role and contribution to neuropsychology and all spoke about the importance of having an Educational Psychologist in their teams.

The specialist contribution of EPs to child neuropsychology was con-ceptualised differently by the EPs working in specialist settings and by the multidisciplinary team members. More specifically, the EPs reflected on how the skills they used in their specialist role were in many respects simi-lar to the "core" EP skills they used in their non-specialist roles, such as systemic thinking and appreciation of the impact of the environment on the child's presentation, as well as their knowledge of the education sys-tem. The healthcare professionals working alongside them highlighted the EP's role as being instrumental in bringing psychological knowledge to the team, as well as knowledge of the educational system. Some practitio-ners noted that the EPs would bridge the gap between health and educa-tion, which no other professional in the team had the skill set and required knowledge to do. For example, while both services had clinical, as well as educational psychologists in their teams, their roles were seen as similar, but distinct. The clinical psychologists were seen as having a key role in facilitating therapeutic interventions for service users with diagnosable mental health conditions, in addition to their broader responsibilities as a psychologist, whereas systemic working and knowledge was seen as the EP's specialist contribution.

This finding appears to challenge the idea that EPs working in neuro-psychological settings engage in activities restricted to administering cog-nitive assessments and have limited scope for systemic work—a misconception encountered by all specialist EPs interviewed for the research. Instead, the results highlighted the input of the EP is highly valued in neuropsychological settings because of the EPs' ability to liaise with a range of professionals and share psychological formulations with the team that take into account the wider systemic context within which the child is positioned. Thus, the EPs unique contribution to neuropsy-chological services can be seen as giving their psychology and education systems knowledge away in order to facilitate systemic thinking in health-care settings.

Moving Forward: How Can EPs Engage with Neuropsychology in an Informed and Ethical Way, Depending on Their Level of Interest, Knowledge and Career Aspirations?

It is hoped this book has highlighted that while EPs may be currently underrepresented in child neuropsychology settings compared to clinical psychologists, they have a key role and place in this specialist area of practice and bring both a unique perspective and a valuable skill set to the field. However, the previous chapters have also pointed to a general sense of confusion and lack of clarity amongst EPs about what neuropsychology theory and practice entail, as well as the different professional development and qualification options in the field of neuropsychology available to them. The complex and multi-component training route to clinical neuropsychology may further contribute to the confusion. For example, completion of the postgraduate diploma or MSc in Clinical Paediatric Neuropsychology may be mistakenly perceived by some to be sufficient in itself to qualify them to practise as a neuropsychologist, as indicated by some national survey responses. Similarly, those unfamiliar with the training and qualification route may not be able to identify the differences in competence, knowledge and the associated limitations to practise between (1) an EP based in a local authority or another community context who occasionally encounters neuropsychological conditions such as epilepsy and acquired brain injury in their work, (2) an EP based in a local authority or another community context who has a specialist interest in neuropsychology and may have completed further study in the area and (3) an EP working in a specialist neuropsychological setting who is not a qualified neuropsychologist and one who *is* a registered neuropsychologist. The following three-tier model presented aims to provide a unified framework for the various levels of engagement with neuropsychology EPs may have depending on their levels of experience, training and interest in the area (Fig. 6.2):

Level 1: Universal Level (All EPs, Regardless of Whether They Have an Interest in Neuropsychology)

Promoting Neuro-Literacy Within the Profession and in Educational Settings
While specialist practice and training in neuropsychology may not be suitable or of interest to all, it is a professional and even an ethical duty for

EPs, regardless of their degree of interest in the neuro-disciplines, to examine their own beliefs and assumptions about brain-based concepts they may have encountered or, indeed, used over the course of their careers. The research findings presented in Chap. 4 suggested that the majority of EPs had not had any formal training or teaching in neuropsychology and their understanding of neuropsychology theory and practice was limited. Yet, many reported using what they understood to be neuropsychology in their practice, as well as making reference to concepts such as "neuroplasticity" and "neuronal pruning", amongst others. While it is not suggested that EPs without formal training in neuropsychology should never use those terms or that they would necessarily be misinterpreting them, it is important to emphasise that even legitimate neuropsychological concepts can be used to justify ideas with a questionable scientific basis. Thus, it may be difficult for professionals, including highly trained ones like EPs, to identify such instances unless they have had appropriate training and knowledge of the field. Similarly, as discussed in Chap. 2, educators who have an interest in science and the brain have been found to be more likely to believe in neuromyths. Therefore, EPs with an interest in neuropsychology, especially if they have not had any formal training in neuropsychology or the neurosciences, should be just as vigilant and cautious when considering claims about the brain as educators and other psychologists with no interest in the area.

Developing Understanding of Common Neuropsychological Conditions Encountered in EP Practice
Promoting neuro-literacy and recognising the limits to one's own competence and knowledge of neuropsychology is an important initial step of engagement for all EPs. However, the research presented in Chap. 4 has highlighted that the majority of EPs, regardless of whether they have an interest in neuropsychology or not, encounter neuropsychological conditions in their everyday practice, with the most commonly encountered ones being epilepsy, acquired brain injury and brain tumours. While the EP's role in a local authority or another community context may not require a *neuropsychological* assessment of the child or young person's needs, all EPs are likely to benefit from developing their knowledge of these conditions and their impact on children and young people's learning, development and socio-emotional wellbeing. Similarly, as discussed in Chap. 3, knowledge of theories such as neuroconstructivism may be particularly helpful for EPs working with children and young people

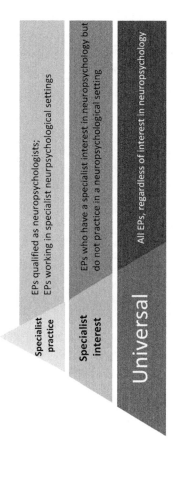

Fig. 6.2 The three-tier model of EPs' engagement with neuropsychology

presenting with a range of neurodevelopmental conditions, including those who may have received multiple diagnoses (i.e. ASD *and* ADHD). Initial training providers and employers such as local authorities are likely to have a key role in facilitating this through teaching and professional development opportunities ideally developed in partnerships with specialist EPs with experience of both maingrade educational psychology casework and neuropsychology practice. These sessions may also provide a suitable opportunity to offer information about the training route into clinical neuropsychology for those EPs who may be considering this specialism option.

Level 2: Specialist Interest Level (EPs Who Have a Specialist Interest in Neuropsychology but Do Not Practise in a Neuropsychological Setting)

This tier refers to EPs who are interested in neuropsychology and may have undertaken additional studies or research in the field (such as the Postgraduate Diploma or MSc in Clinical Paediatric Neuropsychology), but are based in a local authority or another settings with no specific neuropsychological focus. Some EPs in this category may go on to pursue a role in a specialist setting and train as neuropsychologists; however, this may also constitute a separate role in its own right. While it is important to emphasise that EPs at this level of engagement would not be practising as neuropsychologists, they are likely to have a valuable role in bringing neuropsychological knowledge to the community and to local authority educational psychology services. Indeed, considering that the vast majority of local authority-based EPs in the national survey reported that they encounter neuropsychological conditions in their everyday practice, it can be argued that there is a need and a place for EPs with an interest and additional training in neuropsychology in local authority settings. Similarly to other common specialism options available to maingrade EPs (e.g. mental health, autism, early years), a local authority-based EP with a neuropsychology specialism may provide training, support and supervision to colleagues related to neurological or neuropsychological cases they may come across in their day-to-day practice or in the context of Education and Health Care Plan assessments. EPs practising at this level may also have a key role in supporting initial training providers and educational psychology services by taking part in teaching, training and raising awareness of the routes to neuropsychology training.

Level 3: Specialist Practice Level (EPs Qualified as Neuropsychologists and EPs Practising in Neuropsychological Settings)

This tier refers to EPs who are registered neuropsychologists and those who are based in neuropsychological settings but are not qualified neuropsychologists. While some EPs practising in those contexts may be in the process of completing the qualification in clinical neuropsychology, others may prefer to continue to be employed as an "EP in neuropsychology", without pursuing registration as a clinical neuropsychologist but working under the supervision of a registered neuropsychologist. As discussed in Chap. 5, there are a number of factors that may influence the EPs' decision whether to pursue further training or not, such as being happy with their role and responsibilities in their current form or being close to retirement age. Similarly, in some settings, the day-to-day role of the psychologist may not change significantly if they were to complete the qualification, which is another factor that may deter some EPs from pursuing registration. However, it is important to highlight that while these two roles are similar, they are not identical. The qualification in clinical neuropsychology involves a rigorous evaluation process of both knowledge and clinical competence development. At the end of this process, registered neuropsychologists are able to practise autonomously, offer supervision to other qualified or in-training neuropsychologists, as well as take part in expert medico-legal work where a neuropsychological evaluation has been requested by the courts. While EPs are still underrepresented amongst qualified neuropsychologists, EPs' expertise in child development, learning, cognition and knowledge of the education system are highly valued and seen as having a key role in bridging the gap between health and education, as outlined in Chap. 5. Therefore, while this specialist practice area might not be suitable for all EPs, neuropsychology needs to become a more visible professional development option for EPs with an interest in the field.

CONCLUSIONS

Prior to this book and the research presented in it, the relationship between educational psychology and neuropsychology had only been examined explicitly in two theoretical papers, dating back to 15 and 18 years ago (Hood, 2003; MacKay, 2005). While these publications provided an initial exploration of the relationship between the two disciplines and attempted to contextualise it and consider it from multiple perspectives, no attempts to investigate this topic empirically and in more depth have been made since. The research presented in this book has addressed this gap by providing the first empirical examination of the relationship between neuropsychology and educational psychology in the UK, including the emerging specialist role of the EP working in neuropsychological settings. The national survey has improved our understanding of how EPs perceive and apply neuropsychology to their practice and has provided the first examination of EPs' experience of working on neuropsychological cases in their daily practice. Similarly, the interviews with specialist EPs and their colleagues has provided further insight into the role of the EP specialising in neuropsychology, including an exploration of the unique contribution EPs make in neuropsychological settings from multiple perspectives. Additionally, the findings presented in the book have highlighted some potential barriers to the route to qualifying as a clinical neuropsychologist, which are likely to be of particular relevance to the British Psychological Society and the Division of Clinical Neuropsychology.

The book has also highlighted that the majority of qualified EPs (90% of respondents) encounter neurological and neuropsychological conditions in their work, but less than a quarter feel confident about their knowledge in this area. This significant discrepancy has implications for both the professional development options available to EPs post qualification, as well as for initial EP training providers. Universities and EP services may therefore wish to introduce modules or professional development courses with a neuropsychology focus for trainees and staff, the focus of which is on the most commonly encountered neuropsychological conditions by EPs.

Similarly, the research has also challenged some stereotypes about the role of the EP in neuropsychology. Specifically, both the national survey responses and the specialist EPs' experiences suggested that neuropsychology practice is perceived by some as reductionist and overly reliant on psychometric assessments. This view was challenged by the accounts of EPs who reported using neuropsychology in their day-to-day practice to normalise certain behaviours and presentations in children, as well as by the accounts of EPs working in specialist neuropsychological settings. This finding is likely to be of particular relevance to EPs who are interested in neuropsychology, but may be unsure about the focus and scope of the role of the EP in this field.

Additionally, the book has highlighted that the route to qualifying as a clinical neuropsychologist poses a number of obstacles for EPs specialising in neuropsychology, with some deciding not to pursue further training due to the significant financial and time commitments associated with the qualification. Specifically, the BPS-facilitated independent route to qualification was perceived as both more expensive and as providing less structure and support to candidates, compared to the university-facilitated courses covering specific dimensions of the qualifications. The British Psychological Society's Division of Neuropsychology may wish to take these findings into account when reviewing the Qualification in Neuropsychology and particularly the BPS-facilitated independent route. Specifically, it is important to consider that EPs working in neuropsychology undertake the qualification in addition to their other professional duties and responsibilities, and the significant emphasis on self-directed work on the independent route may deter some potential candidates. It may therefore be beneficial for the BPS to explore introducing a structured training route that covers all three dimensions in collaboration with a university in order to avoid fragmentation and confusion of the different routes to qualification.

Another important point emerging from the discussions and research findings presented in the book is that the level of awareness of neuropsychology as a specialism option amongst EPs is very low, yet the role and input of EPs is highly valued in neuropsychology interdisciplinary teams. The BPS and initial EP training providers are likely to have a key role in raising awareness of the availability of this specialism option through the introduction of seminars and talks with EPs specialising in neuropsychology. Chapter 5 in particular can be used as a starting point for this process by providing key information about the role of EPs in neuropsychological settings, common misconceptions, as well as the views of allied healthcare professionals on the EP's role and unique contribution.

Finally, it is hoped that the debates and research findings presented in this book will encourage practitioners to steer clear of extreme positions based on an ideological stance pro or against the neuro-disciplines, rather than ones that are based on evidence. Findings from the neuro-disciplines and their applications to education should be examined with an appropriate level of criticality, given the long history of oversimplification and misrepresentation of neuropsychological and neuroscientific research. However, these should also not be automatically deemed irrelevant, as doing so can restrict and stifle the development of the future relationship between the two disciplines and detract from the significant roles EPs can and do have in child neuropsychology settings. Indeed, the findings highlighted that EPs specialising in neuropsychology are highly regarded professionals with a unique set of skills that make a vital contribution to child neuropsychology settings and bridge the gap between health and education.

REFERENCES

American Academy of Clinical Neuropsychology. (2019, June 28). *Paediatric neuropsychology*. Retrieved from https://theaacn.org/pediatric-neuropsychology/

Ball, H., & Howe, J. (2013). How can educational psychologists support the reintegration of children with an acquired brain injury upon their return to school? *Educational Psychology in Practice, 29*(1), 69–78.

Hale, J. B., & Fiorello, C. A. (2004). *School neuropsychology: A practitioner's handbook*. Guilford Press.

Hood, J. (2003). Neuropsychological thinking within educational psychology. *DECP Debate, 105*, 8–12.

MacKay, T. (2005). The relationship of educational psychology and clinical neuropsychology. *Educational and Child Psychology, 22*(2), 7–17.

National Association of School Psychologists. (2019, June 29). Who are school psychologists. Retrieved from https://www.nasponline.org/about-school-psychology/who-are-school-psychologists

Purves, D., Augustine, G., Fitzpatrick, D., Hall, W., LaMantia, A., White, L., Mooney, R., & Platt, M. (2018). *Neuroscience*. Oxford: Oxford University Press.

Reed, J., & Warner-Rogers, J. (Eds.). (2009). *Child neuropsychology: Concepts, theory, and practice*. John Wiley & Sons.

Reilly, C., & Fenton, V. (2013). Children with epilepsy: The role of the educational psychologist. *Educational Psychology in Practice, 29*(2), 138–151.

REFERENCES

Aaberg, K. M., Gunnes, N., Bakken, I. J., Søraas, C. L., Berntsen, A., Magnus, P., & Surén, P. (2017). Incidence and prevalence of childhood epilepsy: A nation-wide cohort study. *Pediatrics*, e20163908.

Adams, M. P. (2011). Modularity, theory of mind, and autism spectrum disorder. *Philosophy of Science, 78*(5), 763–773.

American Academy of Clinical Neuropsychology. (2019, June 28). *Paediatric neuropsychology*. Retrieved from https://theaacn.org/pediatric-neuropsychology/

Anderson, V., Northam, E., Hendy, J., & Wrennall, J. (2001). *Developmental neuropsychology: A clinical approach*. Hove, UK: Psychology Press.

Anderson, V., Spencer-Smith, M., & Wood, A. (2011). Do children really recover better? Neurobehavioural plasticity after early brain insult. *Brain, 134*(8), 2197–2221.

Annaz, D., Karmiloff-Smith, A., & Thomas, M. S. (2008). The importance of tracing developmental trajectories for clinical child neuropsychology. In J. Reed & J. Warner-Rogers (Eds.), *Child neuropsychology: Concepts, theory and practice* (pp. 7–18). Hoboken: Wiley Blackwell.

Ashton, R. (2015). Educational neuropsychology. In J. Reed, K. Byard, & H. Fine (Eds.), *Neuropsychological rehabilitation of childhood brain injury: A practical guide* (pp. 237–253). London: Springer.

Ball, H., & Howe, J. (2013). How can educational psychologists support the reintegration of children with an acquired brain injury upon their return to school? *Educational Psychology in Practice, 29*(1), 69–78.

Baron, I. S. (2010). Maxims and a model for the practice of pediatric neuropsychology. In K. O. Yeates, M. D. Ris, H. G. Taylor, & B. F. Pennington (Eds.), *Pediatric neuropsychology: Research, theory, and practice* (2nd ed., pp. 473–498). New York, NY: The Guilford Press.

Bartoszeck, A. B., & Bartoszeck, F. K. (2012). How in-service teachers perceive neuroscience as connected to education: An exploratory study. *European Journal of Educational Research, 1*(4), 301–319.

Bear, M. F., Connors, B. W., & Paradiso, M. A. (Eds.). (2007). *Neuroscience (Vol. 2)*. Lippincott Williams & Wilkins.

Bell, G. S., Neligan, A., & Sander, J. W. (2014). An unknown quantity—The worldwide prevalence of epilepsy. *Epilepsia, 55*(7), 958–962.

Bennet, L., Van Den Heuij, L. M., Dean, J., Drury, P., Wassink, G., & Jan Gunn, A. (2013). Neural plasticity and the Kennard principle: Does it work for the preterm brain? *Clinical and Experimental Pharmacology and Physiology, 40*(11), 774–784.

Benton, A. (2000). *Exploring the history of neuropsychology: Selected papers.* New York, NY: Oxford University Press.

Berg, A. T. (2011). Epilepsy, cognition, and behavior: The clinical picture. *Epilepsia, 52,* 7–12.

Besner, D., & Humphreys, G. W. (Eds.). (2012). *Basic processes in reading: Visual word recognition.* Routledge.

Beyerstein, B. (1999). Whence cometh the myth that we only use 10% of our brains? In S. D. Sala (Ed.), *Mind myths. Exploring popular assumptions about the mind and the brain.* John Wiley & Sons.

Blakemore, S. J., & Bunge, S. A. (2012). At the nexus of neuroscience and education. *Developmental Cognitive Neuroscience, 25,* 51–55.

Boyd, R. (2008). Do people only use 10 percent of their brains? *Scientific American.* Retrieved from https://www.scientificamerican.com/article/do-people-only-use-10-percent-of-their-brains/

Bozic, N., & Morris, S. (2005). Traumatic brain injury in childhood and adolescence: The role of educational psychology services in promoting effective recovery. *Educational and Child Psychology, 22*(2), 108–120.

British Psychological Society. (2017). *Qualification in clinical neuropsychology: Candidate handbook.* Retrieved from https://www.bps.org.uk/sites/bps.org.uk/files/Qualifications/QICN%20Candidate %20Handbook%202018.pdf

British Psychological Society. (2018). *Careers in educational psychology.* Retrieved November 14, 2018, from https://careers.bps.org.uk/area/educational

Brooks, B. M., Rose, F. D., Johnson, D. A., Andrews, T. K., & Gulamali, R. (2003). Support for children following traumatic brain injury: The views of educational psychologists. *Disability and Rehabilitation, 25*(1), 51–56.

Bruer, J. T. (1997). Education and the brain: A bridge too far. *Educational Researcher, 26*(8), 4–16.

Cesario, J., Johnson, D. J., & Eisthen, H. L. (2020). Your brain is not an onion with a tiny reptile inside. *Current Directions in Psychological Science*, 0963721420917687.

Chudler, E. H. (2005). *Do we use only 10% of our brain. Neuroscience for kids—10% of the brain myth*. Retrieved February 2, 2012, from http://faculty.washington.edu/chudler/tenper.html

Corballis, M. C. (2007). The dual-brain myth. In S. Della Sala (Ed.), *Tall tales on the brain* (pp. 291–313). Oxford: Oxford University Press.

Costandi, M. (2016). *Neuroplasticity*. MIT Press.

Cramer, S. C., Sur, M., Dobkin, B. H., O'brien, C., Sanger, T. D., Trojanowski, J. Q., & Chen, W. G. (2011). Harnessing neuroplasticity for clinical applications. *Brain, 134*(6), 1591–1609.

Crockard, A. (1996). Confessions of a brain surgeon. *New Scientist, 2061*, 68.

Crowe, L. M., Catroppa, C., Babl, F. E., Rosenfeld, J. V., & Anderson, V. (2012). Timing of traumatic brain injury in childhood and intellectual outcome. *Journal of Pediatric Psychology, 37*(7), 745–754.

Daroff, R. B., Jankovic, J., Mazziotta, J. C., & Pomeroy, S. L. (2015). *Bradley's neurology in clinical practice*. Elsevier Health Sciences.

Davies, H. T. O., Nutley, S. M., & Smith, P. C. (Eds.). (2000). *What works? Evidence-based policy and practice in the public services*. Bristol: Policy Press.

Davis, E. L., Levine, L. J., Lench, H. C., & Quas, J. A. (2010). Metacognitive emotion regulation: Children's awareness that changing thoughts and goals can alleviate negative emotions. *Emotion, 10*(4), 498.

Dekker, S., Lee, N. C., Howard-Jones, P., & Jolles, J. (2012). Neuromyths in education: Prevalence and predictors of misconceptions among teachers. *Frontiers in Psychology, 3*, 429.

Deligiannidi, K., & Howard-Jones, P. A. (2015). The neuroscience literacy of teachers in Greece. *Procedia-Social and Behavioral Sciences, 174*, 3909–3915.

Della Sala, S., & Anderson, M. (Eds.). (2012). *Neuroscience in education: The good, the bad, and the ugly*. Oxford University Press.

Dirks, E., Spyer, G., van Lieshout, E. C., & de Sonneville, L. (2008). Prevalence of combined reading and arithmetic disabilities. *Journal of Learning Disabilities, 41*, 460–473.

Educational Psychology. (2019, April 10). *Educational Psychology*. Retrieved from https://careers.bps.org.uk/area/educational

Epilepsy Action. (2018). Epilepsy facts. Retrieved from https://www.epilepsy.org.uk/press/facts

Epilepsy Society. (2018a). Why do seizures happen?. Retrieved from https://www.epilepsysociety.org.uk/why-do-seizures-happen#.XC0ofmj7SgB

Epilepsy Society. (2018b). Seizure types. Retrieved from https://www.epilepsysociety.org.uk/seizure-types#.XC0oeWj7SgB

Farran, E. K., & Karmiloff-Smith, A. (Eds.). (2012). *Neurodevelopmental disorders across the lifespan: A neuroconstructivist approach.* Oxford University Press.

Fastenau, P. S., Shen, J., Dunn, D. W., & Austin, J. K. (2008). Academic under-achievement among children with epilepsy: Proportion exceeding psychometric criteria for learning disability and associated risk factors. *Journal of Learning Disabilities, 41*(3), 195–207.

Ferrero, M., Garaizar, P., & Vadillo, M. A. (2016). Neuromyths in education: Prevalence among Spanish teachers and an exploration of cross-cultural variation. *Frontiers in Human Neuroscience, 10,* 496.

Fletcher, J. M., Levin, H. S., Lachar, D., Kusnerik, L., Harward, H., Mendelsohn, D., & Lilly, M. A. (1996). Behavioral outcomes after pediatric closed head injury: Relationships with age, severity, and lesion size. *Journal of Child Neurology, 11*(4), 283–290.

Forsyth, R., & Kirkham, F. (2012). Predicting outcome after childhood brain injury. *Canadian Medical Association Journal, 184*(11), 1257–1264.

Gerrans, P. (2003). Nativism and neuroconstructivism in the explanation of Williams syndrome. *Biology and Philosophy, 18*(1), 41–52.

Gibbs, S. (Ed.). (2005). Neuropsychology [Special issue]. *Educational and Child Psychology, 22* (2).

Gilger, J. W., & Kaplan, B. J. (2001). Atypical brain development: A conceptual framework for understanding developmental learning disabilities. *Developmental Neuropsychology, 20*(2), 465–481.

Gilmore, C. K., McCarthy, S. E., & Spelke, E. S. (2007). Symbolic arithmetic knowledge without instruction. *Nature, 447*(7144), 589–591.

Gleichgerrcht, E., Lira Luttges, B., Salvarezza, F., & Campos, A. L. (2015). Educational neuromyths among teachers in Latin America. *Mind, Brain, and Education, 9*(3), 170–178.

Goetz, C. G. (Ed.). (2007). *Textbook of clinical neurology (Vol. 355).* Elsevier Health Sciences.

Goldstein, M. (1994). Decade of the brain. An agenda for the nineties. *Western Journal of Medicine, 161*(3), 239.

Goswami, U. (2006). Neuroscience and education: From research to practice? *Nature Reviews Neuroscience, 7,* 406–413.

Graham, L. (2013). Neuromyths and Neurofacts: Information from cognitive neuroscience for classroom and learning support teachers. *Special Education, 22*(2), 7–20.

Grospietsch, F., & Mayer, J. (2019). Pre-service science teachers' neuroscience literacy: Neuromyths and a professional understanding of learning and memory. *Frontiers in Human Neuroscience, 13,* 20.

Gus, L., Rose, J., & Gilbert, L. (2015). Emotion coaching: A universal strategy for supporting and promoting sustainable emotional and behavioural well-being. *Educational & Child Psychology, 32*(1), 31–41.

Hale, J. B., & Fiorello, C. A. (2004). *School neuropsychology: A practitioner's handbook*. Guilford Press.

Hammersley, M. (2001). *Some questions about evidence-based practice in education. Evidence-based practice in education*. Annual Conference of the British Educational Research Association, University of Leeds, England.

Hammond, P., Hutton, T. J., Allanson, J. E., Buxton, B., Campbell, L. E., Clayton-Smith, J., et al. (2005). Discriminating power of localized three-dimensional facial morphology. *The American Journal of Human Genetics, 77*(6), 999–1010.

Harrison, S., & Hood, J. (2008). Applications of neuropsychology in schools. In J. Reed (Revised J. Warner-Rogers) (Ed.), *Child neuropsychology: Concepts, theory and practice*, (pp. 404–420). Malden, MA: Blackwell.

Headway. (2018). Types of brain injury. Retrieved from https://www.headway.org.uk/about-brain-injury/individuals/types-of-brain-injury/

Hood, J. (2003). Neuropsychological thinking within educational psychology. *DECP Debate, 105*, 8–12.

Horvath, J. C., Donoghue, G. M., Horton, A. J., Lodge, J. M., & Hattie, J. A. (2018). On the irrelevance of neuromyths to teacher effectiveness: Comparing neuro-literacy levels amongst award-winning and non-award winning teachers. *Frontiers in Psychology, 9*, 1666.

Howard-Jones, P. A. (2014). Neuroscience and education: Myths and messages. *Nature Reviews Neuroscience, 15*(12), 817–824.

Howard-Jones, P. A., Franey, L., Mashmoushi, R., & Liao, Y. C. (2009). The neuroscience literacy of trainee teachers. In *British Educational Research Association annual conference* (pp. 1–39). Manchester: University of Manchester.

Hughes, S., Lyddy, F., & Lambe, S. (2013). Misconceptions about psychological science: A review. *Psychology Learning & Teaching, 12*(1), 20–31.

Iversen, S., Berg, K., Ellertsen, B., & Tønnessen, F. E. (2005). Motor coordination difficulties in a municipality group and in a clinical sample of poor readers. *Dyslexia, 11*(3), 217–231.

James, W. (1907). The energies of men. *Science, 25*(635), 321–332.

Jensen, F. E. (2011). Epilepsy as a spectrum disorder: Implications from novel clinical and basic neuroscience. *Epilepsia, 52*, 1–6.

Johnson, M., & de Haan, M. (2015). *Developmental cognitive neuroscience: An introduction*. Blackwell.

Kaplan, B. J., Dewey, D. M., Crawford, S. G., & Wilson, B. N. (2001). The term comorbidity is of questionable value in reference to developmental disorders: Data and theory. *Journal of Learning Disabilities, 34*(6), 555–565.

Kaplan, B., Crawford, S., Cantell, M., Kooistra, L., & Dewey, D. (2006). Comorbidity, co-occurrence, continuum: What's in a name? *Child: Care, Health and Development, 32*(6), 723–731.

Karakus, O., Howard-Jones, P. A., & Jay, T. (2015). Primary and secondary school teachers' knowledge and misconceptions about the brain in Turkey. *Procedia-Social and Behavioral Sciences, 174,* 1933–1940.

Karmiloff-Smith, A. (2009a). Nativism versus neuroconstructivism: Rethinking the study of developmental disorders. *Developmental Psychology, 45*(1), 56.

Karmiloff-Smith, A. (2009b). Preaching to the converted? From constructivism to neuroconstructivism. *Child Development Perspectives, 3*(2), 99–102.

Krätzig, G. P., & Arbuthnott, K. D. (2006). Perceptual learning style and learning proficiency: A test of the hypothesis. *Journal of Educational Psychology, 98*(1), 238.

Lethaby, C., & Harries, P. (2016). Learning styles and teacher training: Are we perpetuating neuromyths? *ELT Journal, 70*(1), 16–27.

Lezak, M. D., Howieson, D. B., Loring, D. W., & Fischer, J. S. (2012). *Neuropsychological assessment.* New York: Oxford University Press.

Macdonald, K., Germine, L., Anderson, A., Christodoulou, J., & McGrath, L. M. (2017). Dispelling the myth: Training in education or neuroscience decreases but does not eliminate beliefs in neuromyths. *Frontiers in Psychology, 8,* 1314.

MacKay, T. (2005). The relationship of educational psychology and clinical neuro-psychology. *Educational and Child Psychology, 22*(2), 7–17.

MacKay, T., Lauchlan, F., Lindsay, G., Monsen, J., Frederickson, N., Gameson, J., & Rees, I. (2016). *Frameworks for practice in educational psychology: A textbook for trainees and practitioners.* Jessica Kingsley Publishers.

MacLean, P. D. (1964). Man and his animal brains. *Modern Medicine, 32,* 95–106.

MacLean, P. D. (1990). *The triune brain in evolution: Role in paleocerebral functions.* Springer Science & Business Media.

Mayer, R. E. (1998). Does the brain have a place in educational psychology? *Educational Psychology Review, 10,* 389–396.

Mayes, S. D., & Calhoun, S. L. (2006). Frequency of reading, math and writing disabilities in children with clinical disorders. *Learning and Individual Differences, 16,* 145–157.

McCabe, D. P., & Castel, A. D. (2008). Seeing is believing: The effect of brain images on judgments of scientific reasoning. *Cognition, 107*(1), 343–352.

Miller, D. C. (Ed.). (2009). *Best practices in school neuropsychology: Guidelines for effective practice, assessment, and evidence-based intervention.* John Wiley & Sons.

National Association of School Psychologists. (2019, June 29). Who are school psychologists. Retrieved from https://www.nasponline.org/about-school-psychology/who-are-school-psychologists

NHS England. (2018). Neurological conditions. Retrieved from: https://www.england.nhs.uk/ourwork/clinical-policy/ltc/our-work-on-long-term-conditions/neurological/

Niogi, S. N., Mukherjee, P., Ghajar, J., Johnson, C. E., Kolster, R., Lee, H., & McCandliss, B. D. (2008). Structural dissociation of attentional control and memory in adults with and without mild traumatic brain injury. *Brain, 131*(12), 3209–3221.

Noble, T., & McGrath, H. (2008). The positive educational practices framework: A tool for facilitating the work of educational psychologists in promoting pupil wellbeing. *Educational and Child Psychology, 25*, 119–134.

O'Hare, A., & Khalid, S. (2002). The association of abnormal cerebellar function in children with developmental coordination disorder and reading difficulties. *Dyslexia, 8*(4), 234–248.

Organisation for Economic Co-operation and Development. (2002). *Understanding the brain: Towards a new learning science*. OECD Publications.

Papadatou-Pastou, M., Haliou, E., & Vlachos, F. (2017). Brain knowledge and the prevalence of neuromyths among prospective teachers in Greece. *Frontiers in Psychology, 8*, 804.

Pasquinelli, E. (2012). Neuromyths: Why do they exist and persist? *Mind, Brain, and Education, 6*(2), 89–96.

Paterson, S. J., Girelli, L., Butterworth, B., & Karmiloff-Smith, A. (2006). Are numerical impairments syndrome specific? Evidence from Williams syndrome and Down's syndrome. *Journal of Child Psychology and Psychiatry, 47*(2), 190–204.

Pei, X., Howard-Jones, P. A., Zhang, S., Liu, X., & Jin, Y. (2015). Teachers' understanding about the brain in East China. *Procedia-Social and Behavioral Sciences, 174*, 3681–3688.

Pietschnig, J., Voracek, M., & Formann, A. K. (2010). Mozart effect–Shmozart effect: A meta-analysis. *Intelligence, 38*(3), 314–323.

Prpic, I., Korotaj, Z., Vlašic-Cicvaric, I., Paucic-Kirincic, E., Valerjev, A., & Tomac, V. (2003). Teachers' opinions about capabilities and behavior of children with epilepsy. *Epilepsy & Behavior, 4*(2), 142–145.

Purves, D., Augustine, G., Fitzpatrick, D., Hall, W., LaMantia, A., White, L., Mooney, R., & Platt, M. (2018). *Neuroscience*. Oxford: Oxford University Press.

Racine, E., Bar-Ilan, O., & Illes, J. (2005). fMRI in the public eye. *Nature Reviews Neuroscience, 6*(2), 159–164.

Racine, E., Bar-Ilan, O., & Illes, J. (2006). Brain imaging: A decade of coverage in the print media. *Science Communication, 28*(1), 122–143.

Rato, J. R., Abreu, A. M., & Castro-Caldas, A. (2013). Neuromyths in education: What is fact and what is fiction for Portuguese teachers? *Educational Research, 55*(4), 441–453.

Rauscher, F. H., Shaw, G. L., & Ky, C. N. (1993). Music and spatial task performance. *Nature, 365*(6447), 611–611.

Rauscher, F. H., Shaw, G. L., & Ky, K. N. (1995). Listening to Mozart enhances spatial-temporal reasoning: Towards a neurophysiological basis. *Neuroscience Letters, 185*(1), 44–47.

Rayner, K., & Pollatsek, A. (2013). *Basic processes in reading*. In D. Reisberg (Ed.), *Oxford library of psychology. The Oxford handbook of cognitive psychology* (pp. 442–461). Oxford University Press. https://doi.org/10.1093/oxfordhb/9780195376746.013.0028

Reed, J., & Warner-Rogers, J. (Eds.). (2009). *Child neuropsychology: Concepts, theory, and practice*. John Wiley & Sons.

Reilly, C., & Fenton, V. (2013). Children with epilepsy: The role of the educational psychologist. *Educational Psychology in Practice, 29*(2), 138–151.

Riener, C., & Willingham, D. (2010). The myth of learning styles. *Change: The Magazine of Higher Learning, 42*(5), 32–35.

Rose, N., & Abi-Rached, J. M. (2013). *Neuro: The new brain sciences and the management of the mind*. Princeton University Press.

Scerif, G., Karmiloff-Smith, A., Campos, R., Elsabbagh, M., Driver, J., & Cornish, K. (2005). To look or not to look? Typical and atypical development of oculomotor control. *Journal of Cognitive Neuroscience, 17*(4), 591–604.

Schoenberg, M. R., & Scott, J: G. (2011). *The little black book of neuropsychology: A syndrome-based approach*. New York: Springer.

Simmonds, A. (2014). *How neuroscience is affecting education: Report of teacher and parent surveys*. Wellcome Trust.

Slomine, B., & Locascio, G. (2009). Cognitive rehabilitation for children with acquired brain injury. *Developmental Disabilities Research Reviews, 15*(2), 133–143.

Specialist Register of Clinical Neuropsychologists. (2020, January 29). Retrieved from https://www.bps.org.uk/lists/SRCN/search?refresh=1

Swiderske, N., Gondwe, J., Joseph, J., & Gibbs, J. (2011). The prevalence and management of epilepsy in secondary school pupils with and without special educational needs. *Child: Care Health and Development, 37*, 96–102.

Tardif, E., Doudin, P. A., & Meylan, N. (2015). Neuromyths among teachers and student teachers. *Mind, Brain, and Education, 9*(1), 50–59.

Teramoto, A., Zuo, H., Zhang, Y., & Kondo, T. (2015). The century of neuroscience. *Translational Neuroscience and Clinics, 1*(2), 73–74.

Thomas, M. S. (2003). Multiple causality in developmental disorders: Methodological implications from computational modelling. *Developmental Science, 6*(5), 537–556.

Tokuhama-Espinosa, T. (2018). *Neuromyths: Debunking false ideas about the brain*. WW Norton & Company.

Trinder, L. (Ed.). (2000). *Evidence-based practice: A critical appraisal*. Oxford: Blackwell Science.

UKABIF. (2018). About brain injury. Retrieved from https://www.ukabif.org. uk/about-brain-injury/

Verger, K., Junqué, C., Jurado, M. A., Tresserras, P., Bartumeus, F., Nogues, P., & Poch, J. M. (2000). Age effects on long-term neuropsychological outcome in paediatric traumatic brain injury. *Brain Injury, 14*(6), 495–503.

Viholainen, H., Ahonen, T., Lyytinen, P., Cantell, M., Tolvanen, A., & Lyytinen, H. (2006). Early motor development and later language and reading skills in children at risk of familial dyslexia. *Developmental Medicine and Child Neurology, 48*(5), 367–373.

Walker, S., & Wicks, B. (2012). *Educating children and young people with acquired brain injury.* Routledge.

Weisberg, D. S., Keil, F. C., Goodstein, J., Rawson, E., & Gray, J. R. (2008). The seductive allure of neuroscience explanations. *Journal of Cognitive Neuroscience, 20*(3), 470–477.

Westermann, G., Mareschal, D., Johnson, M. H., Sirois, S., Spratling, M. W., & Thomas, M. S. (2007). Neuroconstructivism. *Developmental Science, 10*(1), 75–83.

Westermann, G., Thomas, M. S., & Karmiloff-Smith, A. (2010). Neuroconstructivism. In U. Goswami (Ed.), *The Wiley-Blackwell handbook of childhood cognitive development* (pp. 723–748). Chichester: Wiley Blackwell.

Wilding, L., & Griffey, S. (2015). The strength-based approach to educational psychology practice: A critique from social constructionist and systemic perspectives. *Educational Psychology in Practice, 31*(1), 43–55.

Wodrich, D. L., & Cunningham, M. M. (2008). School-based tertiary and targeted interventions for students with chronic medical conditions: Examples from type 1 diabetes mellitus and epilepsy. *Psychology in the Schools, 45*(1), 52–62.

Wodrich, D. L., Jarrar, R., Buchhalter, J., Levy, R., & Gay, C. (2011). Knowledge about epilepsy and confidence in instructing students with epilepsy: Teachers' responses to a new scale. *Epilepsy & Behavior, 20*(2), 360–365.

World Health Organization. (2016). What are neurological disorders? Retrieved from https://www.who.int/news-room/q-a-detail/what-are-neurological-disorders

Wyman, P. A., Cross, W., Brown, C. H., Yu, Q., Tu, X., & Eberly, S. (2010). Intervention to strengthen emotional self-regulation in children with emerging mental health problems: Proximal impact on school behavior. *Journal of Abnormal Child Psychology, 38*(5), 707–720.

Young, A. W., Newcombe, F., Haan, E. H. D., Small, M., & Hay, D. C. (1993). Face perception after brain injury: Selective impairments affecting identity and expression. *Brain, 116*(4), 941–959.

INDEX

© The Author(s), under exclusive license to Springer Nature
Switzerland AG 2020
E. Misheva, *Child Neuropsychology in Practice*,
https://doi.org/10.1007/978-3-030-64930-2

Printed in Great Britain
by Amazon

15735588R00078